Praise for
by Joseph G. Nicholas

"This book tells all. It explains how [hedge funds] work. **THIS IS A SERIOUS AND IMPORTANT BOOK ON THE SUBJECT AND MUST BE READ BY ANY SERIOUS INVESTOR.**"
TradersWorld Magazine

"**NICHOLAS HAS DONE AN INVALUABLE SERVICE** in laying out exactly how hedge funds work, who runs them, how they incorporate, their benefits and risks, and how to go about selecting one."
THE STREET.COM

"For investors who want to learn about hedge funds from A-to-Z, **THIS BOOK IS A MUST-READ.** For those who think they already know about the approximately 4,500 hedge funds with close to $300 billion in assets, **READ THIS BOOK AND LEARN WHAT YOU DON'T KNOW.**"
PETER MORGAN KASH
Senior Managing Director, Paramount Capital Asset Management
Board Member, Hedge Fund Association
Adjunct Professor, Wharton School of Business

"In light of the dramatic increase of investments in hedge funds, the recent media attention, and the widespread need to better understand these complex strategies, **JOE NICHOLAS HAS CREATED A KEY INVESTOR GUIDE TO HEDGE FUNDS,** including the unique and valuable perspective of having top hedge fund managers describe what they do in their own words."
TIMOTHY J. LEACH
Chief Investment Officer
Wells Fargo Private Client Services

"I have yet to find a book **WHICH DOES SUCH A GOOD JOB** of demystifying an area which has been kept deliberately opaque (with good reason) by its players."

AIMA (Alternative Investment Management Association) Newsletter

"Joe Nicholas has written the definitive book on what one needs to know to invest in hedge funds. **IT IS A CLEAR, CONCISE ANALYSIS** of an area that is too often misunderstood. **IT SHOULD BE REQUIRED READING FOR ANYONE CONSIDERING THIS TYPE OF ALTERNATIVE INVESTMENT.**"

CAPPY R. MCGARR
President
McGarr Capital Holdings, LLC

"*Investing in Hedge Funds* is the first comprehensive study of what hedge funds are and how they work. **THIS IS AN ESSENTIAL BOOK FOR ALL INVESTORS CURIOUS ABOUT ALTERNATIVE INVESTMENT STRATEGIES**. Joseph Nicholas details the range of investment strategies pursued by hedge fund managers and writes in a clear, lucid style. **I HIGHLY RECOMMEND THIS BOOK TO ACADEMICS AND PROFESSIONALS WHO WANT TO LEARN ABOUT HEDGE FUNDS.**"

PROFESSOR WILLIAM N. GOETZMANN
Director, International Center for Finance
Yale School of Management

"*INVESTING IN HEDGE FUNDS* **IS A GREAT PRIMER** for anyone looking at our industry. **WELL-RESEARCHED AND CLEARLY WRITTEN**, this comprehensive guide should help both novices and experienced hedge fund investors gain a better understanding of how funds generate their returns and assist them in determining if hedge funds are right for them."

RON POLLACK
Chief Investment Officer
Monitor Fund Advisors, LLC

INVESTING IN

Hedge
FUNDS

Also available from
BLOOMBERG PRESS

Investing in REITs:
Real Estate Investment Trusts
Revised and Updated Edition
by Ralph L. Block

Wall Street Secrets for Tax-Efficient Investing:
From Tax Pain to Investment Gain
by Robert N. Gordon
with Jan M. Rosen

Hedge Fund of Funds Investing:
New Strategies for the Hedge Fund Marketplace
by Joseph G. Nicholas
(May 2003)

Market-Neutral Investing:
Long/Short Hedge Fund Strategies
by Joseph G. Nicholas

The Money-Making Guide to Bonds:
Straightforward Strategies for Picking
the Right Bonds and Bond Funds
by Hildy Richelson and Stan Richelson

A complete list of our titles is available at
www.bloomberg.com/books

BLOOMBERG PERSONAL BOOKSHELF

INVESTING IN

Hedge
FUNDS

Strategies for the New Marketplace

JOSEPH G. NICHOLAS

BLOOMBERG PRESS

PRINCETON

Books are available for bulk purchases at special discounts. Special editions or book excerpts can also be created to specifications. For information, please write: Special Markets Department, Bloomberg Press.

This publication contains the author's opinions and is designed to provide accurate and authoritative information. It is sold with the understanding that the author, publisher, and Bloomberg L.P. are not engaged in rendering legal, accounting, investment-planning, or other professional advice. The reader should seek the services of a qualified professional for such advice; the author, publisher, and Bloomberg L.P. cannot be held responsible for any loss incurred as a result of specific investments or planning decisions made by the reader.

All charts, graphs, and illustrations contained herein were created from data provided by Hedge Fund Research, Inc. All rights reserved. Reprint by permission only.

First edition published 1999

7 9 10 8 6

Nicholas, Joseph G., 1959–
     Investing in hedge funds: strategies for the new marketplace / Joseph G. Nicholas
          p.   cm. – (Bloomberg personal bookshelf)
     Includes bibliographical references and index.
     ISBN 1-57660-060-2
          1. Hedge Funds–United States. I. Title. II. Title: Hedge funds.
III. Series.
HG4930.N53 1999
332.64'5–dc21   98-45960
                                                                          CIP

Book design by Don Morris Design

To my parents
Diana and George Nicholas

ACKNOWLEDGMENTS

I THANK THE FOLLOWING:

For his work on all aspects of the book: Ben Borton.

For their advice, wisdom, and assistance in developing the investment methods and systems discussed in this book, as well as their comments, Mikhail Kimbarovsky and Lori Thompson.

For their insightful help and comments, in good times and bad, on the various strategy chapters we would like to thank the following managers and their staffs: Herb Adler, Jack Barry, Robert Butman, Michelle Day-Gillette and Steve Holtzman, Kate Doyle, Ed Finn and Dan Sido, Ian Hague, Brian Higgins, Randy Jacobis and Paul Upcraft, Dale Jacobs, Russ Kamp, Peter Kash, George Kellner, Dan Knight, Chris Luck, Cappy McGarr, Thomas Noddings and Jerry Van Fleet, Ron Pollack, Paul Siegal, Tim Stack, Ernest Werlin, and Rich Whitman.

For their help building the Hedge Fund Research database: all present and former staff at Hedge Fund Research. For his useful suggestions and assistance in editing, Robert M. Pine. For help with graphics: Mike Miranda. For assistance with manuscript preparation, Michele Anabile. For her patience and encouragement: Jacqueline Murphy at Bloomberg Press.

INTRODUCTION

ROM JANUARY 1990 to March 1998, the hedge fund industry's assets grew twenty fold, from $20 billion to over $400 billion *(see Table 1 on page 4)*[1]. Over the same period, the number of hedge funds increased from 200 to over 3,000 (*see Table 2 on page 5*). Many of us have read periodic reports in the press about hedge funds that generate outsized returns and losses and influence global markets. Most individuals who are familiar with the investment industry know a hedge fund manager or have a friend that does. Some of the biggest names in investing are or were hedge fund managers: George Soros, Julian Robertson, Michael Steinhardt. Increasingly the top minds in finance have left prestigious positions with more traditional funds to start hedge funds. For example, John Meriwether, former Salomon Inc. vice chairman and arbitrage specialist, formed Long-Term Capital Management

Inc. in 1994. Jeff Vinik, who traded Magellan, one of the world's most famous mutual funds, left it to start his own hedge fund in 1996. Jon Jacobson managed part of Harvard's endowment for the better part of the 1990s. When he announced that he was leaving to start a hedge fund, Harvard responded by allocating $500 million to the fund. A greater level of control, the freedom to use almost any financial tool imaginable, and the enormous amount of money that can be made under an incentive-based fee structure are some of the reasons why top talent has made its way to hedge funds. The growth of the industry is obvious. This introduction provides an explanation.

Despite their growing presence in world financial and investment circles, hedge funds are still enveloped in a veil of mystery. Questions abound. What are hedge funds and who runs them? What kind of investment opportunities do they offer and why should I consider

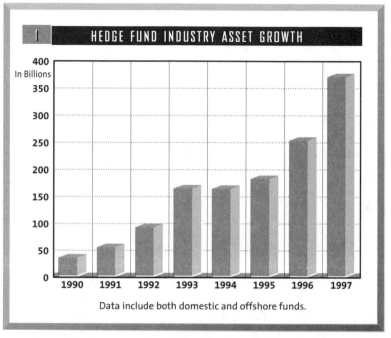

Data include both domestic and offshore funds.

them? What are the benefits and what are the risks? What kind of information do I need and where can I get it? How do I evaluate a hedge fund and how do I invest? What should I look for and what should I avoid?

Whether one ultimately decides to invest in hedge funds and the strategies they pursue, it is important to be informed in order to make an intelligent investment decision. The purpose of this book is to address these questions, share some practical insight into the industry, and provide the investor a starting

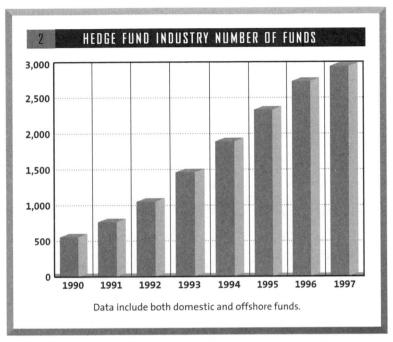

2 HEDGE FUND INDUSTRY NUMBER OF FUNDS

Data include both domestic and offshore funds.

point for making hedge fund investment decisions.

Money managers who distinguish themselves do so not by acting on where profit was generated in the past, but where profit will be generated in the future. Those who correctly anticipate profit potential search in overlooked, complicated, or misunderstood places and employ the tools and techniques necessary to realize them. For the vast majority of investors, the traditional stock and bond investments pursued by individuals, mutual funds, and investment advisory firms represent where the investment community is now. But regulation and tradition restrict the investment approaches they employ in ways that limit the investment strategies and opportunities they can pursue. A private investment industry has advanced onto the global investment scene to profit from nontraditional opportunities. Some of the world's most sophisticated investors fund the industry, and their money is managed by a group of talented and savvy money managers who pursue a broad spectrum of alternative investment strategies. The assets are pooled and managed in private investment structures called hedge funds.

Assets are flowing to hedge funds at an increasing rate because institutions and individuals alike see hedge funds as an integral part of their overall investment approach. By providing exposures that investors may not already have, hedge funds allow these investors to further diversify their investment portfolios, protect against risks inherent in traditional stock market approaches, and realize excess returns. The specialized strategies that hedge fund managers employ provide access to markets around the globe. But, they do not all pursue the same investment approach or provide the same exposures.

Some provide lower risk alternatives to traditional investments; others, through the use of leverage, take outsized risks in search of large gains. They may specialize in long term investment approaches, arbitrage opportunities, or short term trading strategies. Some make profits as markets rise and some as markets fall. Some provide protection against market declines or neutralize certain market risks. Others magnify the exposure to various markets.

Hedge fund managers are entrepreneurs who establish specialized money management firms. Expanding global markets provide plenty of areas where they can mine profits. By harnessing the power of computers and information technology, and applying their skill and expertise toward identifying profit opportunities, they provide a method to access these potential returns. An increasing amount of information is available at decreasing cost. At the same time, we are in the midst of a period of global economic and political change unparalleled in history. As global markets expand and become increasingly complex, inefficiencies emerge which create specialized opportunities for investors. Many hedge fund strategies are utilized by small specialist shops that a decade or two ago could not have used them, because the information required to exploit these inefficiencies was only available at a high cost that only the larger brokerage and investment firms could afford. Real time information and technological progress have allowed numerous small money management operations to use hedge fund strategies to take advantage of market inefficiencies created by the changing global economy.

New markets and financial instruments have emerged and will grow in response to changes driven by technology and the needs of increasingly sophisticated global investors. Financial futures were created in the 1970s, mortgage-backed securities in the 1980s, and the Russian emerging market was created in the 1990s. These kinds of changes in markets and financial instruments create complexities and pricing uncertainties and thus profit opportunities that managers employing alternative investment strategies are well equipped to capitalize on.

Alternative investment strategies allow hedge fund managers to capitalize on market inefficiencies created by rapid global economic change in a way that traditional long term investment strategies cannot. Because mutual funds are highly regulated, they have been restricted in their use of certain instruments and investment techniques such as leveraging and derivatives trading. These regulations limit the risk exposure that a mutual fund can have, but also make it difficult to outperform the market or to protect against a general market decline because their primary investment tool is the ability to pick good stocks and bonds. Hedge funds, on the other hand, are not subject to the same restrictions and can use nontraditional techniques and instruments to protect against and profit from such market movements.

Most hedge fund managers are specialized to some degree and restrict themselves to a particular strategy. They attract investors by exhibiting a high level of expertise in that strategy. Today, the majority of hedge funds are run by managers who pursue high risk-adjusted returns for their clients by creating informational, statistical, or strategic advantages that allow them to turn market inefficiencies into profits.

It is no secret to the investment community that market inefficiencies represent profit opportunities. Markets always seek to become efficient, but they have—and will continue to have—inefficiencies. In spite of this, the notions of perfect information, perfect competition, and theoretical equilibrium still haunt investors' thoughts, even though they are concepts that exist only in the pages of introductory economics texts. In actuality, market disequilibrium—which requires a certain level of market inefficiency—is, as George Soros once said, "inherent in the imperfect understanding of the participants." He went on to say that, "financial markets are inherently unstable, and the idea of a theoretical equilibrium . . . is itself a product of our imperfect understanding."[2] The point is that as long as it takes time to communicate information, there will be information gaps, or inefficiencies, that result in a difference between the "real" or potential value of an asset and its market value. Hedge fund managers use informational, statistical, or strategic advantages to make intelligent, informed estimates of the real value of assets; take positions in those assets whose market value differs from their estimate; hedge out extraneous risk; and reap the returns when information about the asset becomes more readily available and the market reacts accordingly.

A great number of factors have contributed to the rapid growth of both hedge funds and hedge fund assets. Here are five that have been the most important:

1 **Opportunity.** The continuing expansion of global markets and the ongoing development of new markets provides an expanding arena for investments. As long as economic conditions change and information flows imperfectly, markets will have inefficiencies. Markets are always striving to correct these inefficiencies because they represent profit opportunities. But while they remain, astute

investment managers operating through the hedge fund investment vehicle provide investors with a way to capitalize on such inefficiencies.

2 Tools and support services. New investment instruments and brokerage services continue to evolve and to become broadly available. The technology explosion has resulted in a rapid increase in the amount of information available to investors and the timeliness of that data. Likewise, ongoing increases in computing power allow market participants to analyze and process this information more quickly and more thoroughly. At the same time the cost of such products and services has been drastically reduced.

3 Talent and expertise. As a result of the reduced cost of investment instruments, returns have become less dependent on large and costly infrastructure and the value of talented individuals has increased. One person with a personal computer can command more informational resources and analytical power today than was possible by an investment division on Wall Street in the mid-1980s. The human factor is a key to successfully applying investment capital to current opportunities. Investment funds naturally flow to those money managers who can offer specialized knowledge, expertise, and flat-out investment talent.

4 Favorable markets. The 1990s' bull market has helped the hedge fund industry as well as traditional investments. Because of the enormous amount of wealth that was created during that decade, hedge fund managers have found it easier to obtain initial investment capital. It often originates from family and friends interested in investing a few million to back a new money management firm. The environment has also been conducive to the incubation of new investment businesses. Because many hedge fund managers have been able to generate profits early on, and so earn a percentage of the profits, a larger number of hedge funds have survived than would have in a less favorable market. To illustrate the point, consider that hedge fund managers earn 20 percent of the profits they generate. A new manager with $10 million under management that generates a 20 percent return earns $400,000.

If the year were flat the business would earn only the 1 percent management fee, hardly enough to operate a new business for very long. A wealthier populace also means a larger potential investor base for private investments such as hedge funds. They are exempt from publicly registering their securities, but the exemption generally limits them to wealthy, or accredited, investors. However, the definition of who qualifies as a wealthy or accredited investor was written over half a century ago. Needless to say, the number of persons that qualify is significantly greater than at the time of drafting and continues to expand.

5 Performance. Even with all other factors, the industry would not grow without producing results. With few exceptions, the investment strategies pursued by hedge fund managers have generated attractive risk adjusted returns.

THE STRUCTURE OF THIS BOOK

CHAPTER 1 ADDRESSES the question: what is a hedge fund? The term has no formal definition and is used interchangeably to describe both an investment structure and an investment approach. At the outset of the chapter is a terse, boxed definition followed by a deeper look into the ideas that underpin the concept. A brief look into the past provides some historical context, but the key to understanding hedge funds lies in separating the structure of the investment from the alternative investment strategy the fund manager employs. A hedge fund is not a static entity. It is a structure that allows the different components of the hedge fund world to interact. The most important components are the investment structure or vehicle, the investor, the fund manager, and the investment strategy. The interaction between these components forms the hedge fund dynamic. The second half of this chapter sketches out the broad outlines of these major components and then presents a diagram to help readers understand how the interaction between the major components forms one dynamic process.

Chapter 2 discusses the hedge fund structures that allow hedge fund managers to use a wider variety of innovative investment strategies than more traditional forms of investment. In the past, the term *hedge fund* cryptically described both an investment vehicle—a commingled investment fund—and a strategy of long and short stock investing incorporating leverage. Today, it only describes investment fund structures such as limited partnerships and offshore corporations that allow access to the various hedge fund strategies. The regulatory framework and available legal entities drive the types of investment structures that investors will use. The important features of hedge fund structures potential investors need to consider are covered in this chapter, including: legal forms, associated documentation such as limited partnership agreements, offering memorandum and subscription materials, registration and regulation, fees and expenses, investment size, lockup periods, liquidity, performance and reporting, tax issues, and ERISA (Employee Retirement Income Security Act) considerations.

Chapter 3 is an introduction to the most prominent hedge fund strategies. It introduces the elements of investing that make up these approaches. This

introduction is intended to provide readers a
framework for understanding and comparing
different strategies. Many elements are not vastly
different from those that make up traditional investing
strategies. What is different is how the practitioners
of each strategy weigh the various elements in
combination with new elements and incorporate long
and short exposures. Roughly, there are five important groups of elements: 1 tools and techniques,
2 instruments and markets, 3 sources of return,
4 measures for controlling risk, and 5 performance.
How different strategies weight these elements
determines the risk/reward characteristics that each
strategy aims to produce. The second half of the
chapter introduces the universe of the eleven
prominent hedge fund strategies covered in more
detail in later chapters. Each of the eleven strategies
is described briefly with a graph illustrating the asset
growth of hedge funds in the 1990s and the returns
those funds have produced. Following is a consideration of the universe as a whole in terms of assets
under management and risk/reward profiles. By the

end of this chapter, readers should have a broad sense of the spectrum of hedge fund choices and be ready for the more detailed examinations of the different approaches that follow in the individual strategy chapters.

Chapters 4 through 14 describe how the practitioners of each hedge fund strategy produce returns and control risk. Each strategy is described in terms of core strategic propositions, investment process, performance, advantages, and disadvantages. While the overall goal of this book is to assist hedge fund investors in their understanding hedge fund strategies, each strategy chapter is also designed to stand alone. The reader with interest in a particular strategy should not become lost by reading one chapter in isolation.

Chapter 15 suggests a framework for selecting hedge funds and alternative investment strategies for investment allocation. It is written for investors who want to construct a multiple manager portfolio, but the concepts can be applied to a single manager or hedge fund as well. Three basic interrelated steps or stages in making an allocation to hedge funds are discussed: 1 planning the investment, 2 selecting the optimal structure and appropriate strategies, and 3 searching for and selecting the best managers.

Chapter 16 offers more detail on due diligence and describes three issues that affect hedge fund investors after they make an initial allocation: 1 ongoing due diligence, 2 portfolio transparency, and 3 risk monitoring. These disclosure issues have become more important as institutional investors with fiduciary responsibilities have begun to allocate assets to hedge funds. In light of the unexpected losses experienced by a number of secretive funds in 1998, prudence dictates that investors use risk monitoring systems that provide protection through some level of control over the investment.

The Epilogue describes where hedge funds are headed, and some developments to expect in the near future.

KEYS TO
Understanding

CHAPTER

1

What Is a
HEDGE
FUND?

HEDGE FUND describes an investment structure for managing a private unregistered investment pool. This structure charges an incentive-based fee that compensates the fund manager through a percentage of the profits that the fund earns. Exemption from securities registration limits the number of participants who must also be accredited investors or institutional investors. All hedge funds are not alike; managers usually specialize in one of a diverse number of alternative investment strategies operated through the hedge fund structure.

IN THE PAST, the term *hedge fund* described both an investment structure—a commingled investment fund—and a strategy—a leveraged long portfolio "hedged" by stock short sales. Today, it only describes the investment structure. Like the term *mutual fund,* which describes only the investment structure and does not indicate whether it invests in stocks or bonds or in the United States or abroad, the term *hedge fund* does not tell an investor anything about the underlying investment activities. A hedge fund acts as a vehicle, helping an investor get to the ultimate investment goal: to turn market opportunities into investment returns. In this respect, a hedge fund is no different from a mutual fund. Hedge funds differ from mutual funds in the range of allowable investment approaches, the goals of the strategies that they use, and in the breadth of tools and techniques available to investment managers to achieve those goals for investors. (It should be noted that this distinction is becoming blurred. Mutual fund regulatory changes have allowed certain hedge fund strategies to operate under the mutual fund structure.)

Since the term *hedge fund* describes an investment structure, not an investment approach, to understand hedge funds it is necessary to separate the structure of the investment from the investment strategy.

The *investment structure* is the legal entity that allows investment assets to be pooled and permits the hedge fund manager to invest them. The investment approach that the manager takes is known as the *hedge fund strategy* or *alternative investment strategy*. The structure establishes such things as the method of manager compensation, the number and type of investors, and the rights and responsibilities of investors regarding profits, redemptions, taxes, and reports. The elements that make up the strategy include how the manager invests, which markets and instruments are used, and which opportunity and return source is targeted.

HEDGE FUND HISTORY

AS SURPRISING AS it may sound, some hedge fund strategies do not involve hedging. Although many strategies allow managers to use both long and short investments, some do not. A review of the strategies used by hedge fund managers today shows that, for some, the lineage stretches back to the activities of Benjamin Graham's investment activities of the 1920s. The term *hedge fund,* however, is said to have originated in 1949 when Alfred Winslow Jones combined a leveraged long stock position with a portfolio of short stocks in an investment fund with an incentive fee structure. Although some have argued that the Jones-style hedge fund is the only true one, the term is now universally used to describe the housing for a diverse range of underlying investment strategies.

In 1966, *Fortune* magazine published an article by Carol Loomis entitled "The Jones Nobody Keeps Up With" *(see sidebar)* that highlighted Jones's hedge fund.

Loomis's article shocked the investment community by showing that Jones's relatively unknown hedge fund outperformed all the mutual funds of its time. The best mutual fund over the prior five years had been the Fidelity Trend Fund, but Jones's fund outperformed it by 44 percent. The

THE JONES NOBODY KEEPS UP WITH

THERE ARE REASONS to believe that the best professional manager of investors' money these days is a quiet-spoken, seldom photographed man named Alfred Winslow Jones. Few businessmen have heard of him, although some with long memories may remember his articles in *Fortune;* he was a staff writer in the early 1940s. In any case, his performance in the stock market in recent years has made him one of the wonders of Wall Street—and made millionaires of several of his investors. On investments left with him during the five years ended last May 31 (when he closed his 1965 fiscal year), Jones made 325 percent. Fidelity Trend Fund, which had the best record of any mutual fund during those years, made "only" 225 percent. For the ten-year period ended in May, Jones made 670 percent; Dreyfuss Fund, the leader among mutual funds that were in business all during that decade, had a 358 percent gain.

The vehicle through which Jones operates is not a mutual fund but a limited partnership. Jones runs two such partnerships, and they have slightly different investment objectives. In each case, however, the underlying investment strategy is the same: the fund's capital is both leveraged and "hedged." The leverage arises from the fact that the fund margins itself to the hilt; the hedge is provided by short positions—there are always some in the fund's portfolio.

Jones's accomplishments have spawned a number of other "hedge funds."

— *Carol J. Loomis*
Fortune Magazine [3]

best mutual fund over the prior ten years had been the Dreyfuss Fund, but Jones's fund outperformed it by a whopping 87 percent. The article was widely read, and enterprising investors tried to imitate Jones's fund. The number of hedge funds quickly jumped from a handful to more than a hundred. However, the majority of the new managers were seduced by the lure of incentive-based fees and leverage in a bull market and quickly abandoned the time-consuming, risk-reducing process of hedging a portfolio with short sales. As a result, in the bust years of the early 1970s, many of the more inexperienced fund managers suffered significant losses and had to exit the hedge fund industry. Survivors of this first spate of attrition, such as George Soros and Michael Steinhardt, went on to become some of the largest hedge fund managers in the industry.

It is important to note that Jones came up with a novel and successful investment strategy. However, to pool investor assets he needed a structure, and because the public mutual fund structure did not accommodate the requirements of the strategy, he used the private limited partnership instead. When hedge fund managers decided to pool monies offshore, they also used private investment structures that incorporated many of the same features.

As the more successful hedge fund managers' assets under management grew, some of them changed their approach. In the 1970s and 1980s, managers with roots in stock picking sought opportunities in broader global markets: fixed-income securities, foreign exchange, equities, and commodities. Because they retained the private investment structure that allowed them to maintain the ability to go long or short and to use leverage, the term *hedge fund* stuck with them in discussions of the investment pool. The strategy that they used, however, was described as "global macro," "global opportunistic," or just "macro."

At the same time, computerization, information technology, new markets, and investment instruments such as options, futures, and swaps created new opportunities for smaller specialized money management firms. In putting together private investment pools, the hedge fund model was adopted, as was its name, by both managers and investors alike. But the underlying strategy that the manager used included any one of a number of existing or new approaches, such as fixed-income arbitrage, equity-market-neutral investing, or event-driven investing. The unifying element of hedge funds is its structure.

HEDGE FUND STRUCTURE

HEDGE FUNDS ARE usually structured as private investment pools. The actual legal entity (limited partnership,
corporation, trust, mutual fund) depends on where the
fund is domiciled (legally located) and the type of
investors that it seeks to attract. In the United States, these
usually take the form of a limited partnership, whereas
outside the United States, or "offshore," they may assume
corporate or other investment company forms. In contrast
to mutual funds, which are structured as public investment
companies, hedge funds are private. This means that the
securities that they offer to investors are exempt from
being publicly registered with the Securities and Exchange
Commission (SEC), although they still must satisfy certain
disclosure obligations in the offering of the securities and
must comply with SEC antifraud provisions. The exemption that allows hedge funds to remain private also limits
the number and type of investors allowed. In most cases,
an investor must be either an institution or an individual
classified as accredited or higher. An **ACCREDITED
INVESTOR** is **1** an individual who has made $200,000 a
year in income for the past two years and has a reasonable
expectation of doing so in the future; **2** one who, together
with a spouse, has an income of $300,000 per year; or
3 one who has a net worth of $1 million, excluding home
and automobile. The individual exemption limits the
number of investors to ninety-nine, requiring a manager
to establish a high minimum investment to accumulate a
reasonable amount of assets. Minimums usually range
from $100,000 to $5 million.

The difference between mutual funds and most hedge
funds can be seen in their different approaches to fee
structures, liquidity, asset valuation, and disclosure of
information. Whereas mutual funds charge an ongoing
percentage fee based on the amount of assets invested,
hedge funds charge both an asset-based fee and an incentive fee. The asset-based fee, called the *management fee,* is

usually 1 percent per annum, charged monthly or quarterly. The incentive fee, also called a *carried interest,* gives the hedge fund manager a percentage of the profits earned by the fund. Incentive fees range from 10 to 30 percent but are normally 20 percent of annual profit. Hedge funds are also less liquid than mutual funds. Although mutual funds offer daily liquidity, U.S. hedge funds often require a lockup period of up to one year or more, although offshore funds may allow monthly or quarterly exits. Lockup periods are necessary because many of the alternative investment strategies that hedge fund managers use are long term in nature and do not provide ongoing liquidity. In addition, certain securities laws that prohibit the collection of incentive fees for less than a twelve-month period affect hedge funds. Hedge funds and mutual funds also differ in the way that their portfolios are valued. Mutual funds are valued daily with a published net asset value (NAV) In most cases, U.S. hedge funds provide investors only a monthly estimate of percentage gain or loss. Offshore funds may offer NAV form reporting, although it is usually on a monthly basis. In any case, information about mutual funds is more readily available than that about hedge funds. Because of their public status, mutual funds are required to disclose certain financial information. Hedge funds, however, have no obligation to disclose their information publicly. Even investors themselves often have only limited access to information, although this is changing as hedge fund managers increasingly move to attract and accommodate institutional investors.

HEDGE FUND STRATEGIES

THERE IS NOTHING mystical about the strategies that hedge fund managers use. These strategies can be described in the same terms as those for a traditional portfolio: return source, investment method, buy/sell process, market and instrument concentrations, and risk control. The alternative investment strategies that hedge fund managers tend to use produce returns by leveraging some kind of informational or strategic advantage. Essentially, although some hedge fund strategies are complex, hedge fund investing can be understood by anyone familiar with financial markets and instruments who also has a basic working knowledge of corporate structure and finance.

Although it is important to acknowledge that most money managers who operate private investment pools using the hedge fund structure have their own styles, most of these specialized investment approaches can be categorized within the list of general strategies described in this book. The hedge fund universe is composed of managers who use a broad range of variations of these strategies. These strategies may have little or nothing in common except that they operate under the hedge fund structure and are considered to be alternatives to traditional investment approaches.

Alternative investments differ from the traditional investment approaches used in mutual funds in many significant ways. Traditional investment strategies are exclusively long. Their practitioners seek stocks or bonds that they think will outperform the market. However, alternative investment strategies invest long, short, or both, combining two or more instruments to create one investment position. Traditional strategies do not take advantage of leverage. Some alternative strategies do.

Many alternative strategies make use of hedging techniques. Unlike traditional strategies that lose money in a market decline, hedged strategies will generate profit on their hedges to offset all or a portion of the market losses. Hedging may take a number of forms, depending on the strategy. Some hedges seek to generate profit on an on-going basis; others may be purely defensive or insurance against market crashes. In general, they are positions that will profit in a market decline by providing an offset, or hedge, to losses incurred on investments in the portfolio that are exposed to the market.

The returns generated by traditional long-only strategies are relative, or benchmarked, to market indices. For exam-

ple, if a traditional mutual fund invests in large-capitalization U.S. equities, its return is benchmarked to the performance of a large-capitalization stock index, and performance is judged relative to that index. Most alternative
strategies, however, target absolute returns. Because the
source of return for most of these strategies is not based on
market direction and does not relate to a particular market
or index, it is not useful to compare returns with a traditional market index. Rather, returns are expected to fall
within a certain range, regardless of what the markets do.

The hedge fund strategies covered in this book are dif-
ferentiated by the tools used and the profit opportunities
targeted. The different strategies have very different
risk/reward characteristics, so it is important that potential investors distinguish between them instead of lump-
ing them together under the heading of "hedge funds."
Hedge funds are heterogeneous. To render them comparable, they must be categorized by the core strategy that
the fund manager uses. Some hedge fund strategies, such
as macro funds, use aggressive approaches, whereas
others, such as nonleveraged market-neutral funds, are
conservative. Many have significantly lower risk than a traditional portfolio of long stocks and bonds for the same
levels of return.

HEDGE FUND MANAGERS

HEDGE FUND MANAGERS are more difficult to categorize
than the various strategies of the funds they manage. Their
diverse backgrounds often provide them with the specialized knowledge, expertise, and skills they use to implement unique variations of general strategies.

The typical hedge fund manager is an entrepreneur
who organizes a money management company and investment fund to pool the manager's assets (often a substantial portion of his or her net worth) with those of family,
friends, and other investors. The manager's primary
efforts are directed toward the implementation of a hedge
fund strategy and the management of a profitable invest-

ment portfolio. Often, the "business culture" of the manager and the money management company will reflect these primary efforts, with less emphasis on selling and investor relations when compared with traditional investment operations. Since hedge fund managers are investing their own assets along with those of the other investors, they are highly motivated to achieve investment returns and to reduce risk. This motivation has translated into success, as evidenced by the significant growth of the hedge fund industry and the proliferation of hedge funds and managers. Increasingly, institutions and traditional money management firms are organizing internal operations to pursue hedge fund strategies by converting traditional managers and training new ones.

HEDGE FUND INVESTORS

HEDGE FUND INVESTORS have traditionally been high-net-worth individuals. At times, more than half of these were from countries outside the United States. These non-U.S. investors sought to invest with the top investment talent, which was almost exclusively based in the United States. Recently, the increasing number of American and international high-net-worth individuals has been joined by institutional investors, including pension funds, endowments, banks, and insurance companies. An infrastructure has emerged to process and make available information about hedge funds. In light of these developments, institutions have become more open to exploring allocations to alternative investment strategies. In response, many hedge funds have made changes, such as providing transparency, to accommodate the needs of institutional investors. It has been a self-reinforcing process: as funds make information about their operations available to institutions, infrastructure to support this body of information is created, and institutions are more likely to make allocations to hedge funds. Although these institutional investors represent a small number of hedge fund investors, they control large amounts of assets and usually make much larger allocations than individuals; thus funds are willing to accommodate their needs.

THE HEDGE FUND DYNAMIC

AS STATED EARLIER, the hedge fund structure is an investment vehicle because it helps investors reach their ultimate goal: to turn market opportunities into investment returns. The investor brings funds to the industry. These assets are pooled in investment structures called hedge funds. The investment structure gives the investor access to hedge fund managers who provide investment expertise and use alternative investment strategies. For investors, the hedge fund structure is both a method to pool their assets with those of other investors and a way to access talented hedge fund managers, the alternative investment strategies they use, and the exposures they provide. For managers, the structure enables them to pool the assets of wealthy investors, allows them to implement their particular strategies, and permits them to collect an incentive-based fee from their investors. They combine their expertise with an alternative investment strategy to generate returns for their investors and for themselves, completing the dynamic.

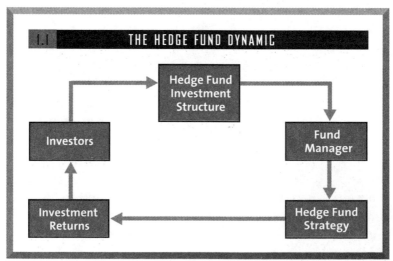

1.1   THE HEDGE FUND DYNAMIC

CHAPTER

The Hedge Fund
INVESTMENT
STRUCTURE

N INVESTOR CAN access a hedge fund manager in one of two ways: **1** by investing in an existing investment vehicle or **2** by placing assets in a separate managed account and hiring the hedge fund manager to invest them. A hedge fund, like a mutual fund, is an investment vehicle that allows multiple investors to pool their assets and enables them to access hedge fund managers' specialized knowledge, investment expertise, and innovative trading strategies. Like the strategies that hedge fund managers use, not all hedge funds are alike. Nevertheless, many features with which an investor should be familiar before investing in a hedge fund can be usefully discussed in general terms. This chapter first discusses the differences between existing investment vehicles and separate managed accounts. It then examines some of the features of hedge fund structures: the legal form of both domestic and offshore funds, documentation, registration and regulation, fees and expenses, investment size, lockup periods, performance reporting, tax issues, and Employment Retirement Income Security Act (ERISA) considerations.

EXISTING INVESTMENT VEHICLES

IN THE UNITED STATES, most hedge funds are limited partnerships. Investors become limited partners by purchasing interests in the partnership. The general partner of a limited partnership may be an individual or corporate entity. In the case of hedge funds, the general partner is often the fund manager, who will have a large portion of his or her net worth invested in the fund that he or she manages. The general partner's liability is unlimited, but the other partners provide compensation through fees linked to the fund's performance. Typically, the manager receives 1 percent of the fund's total assets annually and 20 percent of the profits. One of the distinguishing features of hedge funds is this incentive fee structure. The partnership's profits, losses, and tax consequences "flow through" to the investors.

Four of every five hedge fund managers are based in the United States. The terms *onshore* and *offshore* are commonly used to designate where the fund is organized for legal and tax purposes (its domicile). Hedge funds that are organized outside the United States are called "offshore" funds. Offshore funds are typically established in the Caribbean tax havens, and they are usually organized as corporations. Investors purchase shares in the corporation in the same way as they would purchase shares in a mutual fund; but the minimum required contribution is much higher, and many funds limit the number of contributors. The fund's gains and losses do not flow through to the investor; rather they are realized when the share price of the fund's stock appreciates or depreciates.

Both onshore and offshore managers do not typically disclose the contents of funds' portfolios to their investors, although access to this information, called transparency, is increasing and is demanded by many investors. Managers report on performance on a limited basis—for most funds, this means monthly and for some others, quarterly. In addition, some fund managers require that investors "lock up" their assets for a certain period of time, which means that existing hedge fund vehicles can be illiquid investments.

Nearly all U.S. hedge funds limit their investors to the Securities and Exchange Commission's (SEC) definition of an accredited investor. Minimum investment requirements range from $100,000 to $5 million and normally fall within the $500,000 to $1 million range. In general, funds accepting new investors will open on a monthly or quarterly basis. Investors who cannot meet the minimum investment size for a domestic or offshore fund sometimes participate through a feeder fund structure or wrap fee program. Basically, these arrangements enable pooling of multiple investors to meet a minimum investment size target. In a feeder fund structure, two levels of fees are imposed—one at the feeder fund level and one at the underlying fund level. As a result, fees are typically higher than in a single-tier structure. In a wrap fee program, the program sponsor compensates the individual hedge fund managers who participate. Fees paid by investors to the wrap fee sponsor include compensation to the sponsor and the compensation that will be passed through to the hedge fund manager. As with a feeder fund, the total level of fees is higher than in a single-tier structure.

SEPARATE MANAGED ACCOUNTS

ALTHOUGH A MANAGED or separate account is not a hedge fund, it is a method for accessing the investment talents of hedge fund managers. Rather than investing in an existing fund, an investor can place assets in a separate account and hire a hedge fund manager as an investment adviser to invest them on a discretionary basis. Not all hedge fund managers will do this. Multiple separate accounts create administrative burdens that the manager may or may not be willing to take on (individual reports, transparency requirements, specialized liquidity demands, trade allocation issues, individualized investment strategies, increased likelihood of requirement to register as an investment adviser). If the manager is willing to take on an individual account, the required minimum amount is usually large ($3 million to $25 million), although certain managers are set up to operate smaller accounts. Sometimes, fund managers will prefer to use a managed account structure—for example, when the manager must develop a performance record to attract a sufficient number of investors to justify the expense of forming a fund.

A managed account is an active investment vehicle that allows the investor to retain custody and control over his or her assets. In contrast to the preset terms of existing structures, all aspects of the private investment advisory relationship are potentially negotiable, allowing the investor to be very involved in the investment details. For example, an investor who proposes to make a large investment may insist on a managed account to facilitate a better fee structure and more liberal withdrawal terms than are offered to fund investors generally. Sometimes, the investor pays only an asset management fee—typically 1 to 2 percent of the net asset value (NAV) of the account. In other cases, the client also pays a performance fee based on increases in NAV—typically 10 to 20 percent. Generally, no performance fee is payable until the client has recouped past losses. In addition, existing funds usually use a single investment strategy and do not customize their operations to meet the needs of individual fund investors. Therefore, if an investor wants a different investment program than the one the fund proposes to use, a separate managed account may be preferable. In a fund, no one investor has the power to change the strategy, but managed accounts enable investors to dictate changes in the investment program over time.

The investor and the hedge fund manager will negotiate an agreement that details the nature of the separate managed account. The agreement specifies the types of investments that may be made by the manager. Some agreements are nondiscretionary—the client must approve investments. Other agreements are discretionary—the portfolio manager can make investments without client preclearance, provided that they conform to the guidelines set forth in the agreement. Investment restrictions may include, among other things: caps on the portion of the account that may be invested in a single issuer or industry or type of investment strategy (e.g., health care, emerging markets) or type of instrument (e.g., bonds, commodities, derivatives); restrictions on investment in assets in which the investor has a conflict of interest; and lists of permitted short-term investments (e.g., Treasury bills, certificates of deposit). Sometimes, the investor reserves the right to change the investment approach at any time. Usually, the investor agrees to leave the account with the manager for a fixed minimum period of time (lockup period) unless the manager breaches the agreement or causes more than the specified level of loss.

On the downside, the investor theoretically has unlimited liability, but this can be controlled by setting up an intermediary corporation, creating, in effect, a private fund. The investor can often choose from different investment programs or strategies that the fund manager uses, or the account may be customized to provide specific exposures. A managed account is considered quite liquid because the investor can typically terminate the account at short notice. Managed accounts are usually held with a custodian, and the trades are typically executed and cleared by independent brokers. The investor receives copies of all transactions and has full knowledge of all the account's positions. This ability to see through an investment vehicle to the contents of the portfolio is called transparency. Fully transparent managed accounts give investors a greater degree of control over their investment but also increase the amount of administrative work for the manager and fees incurred by the investor. The

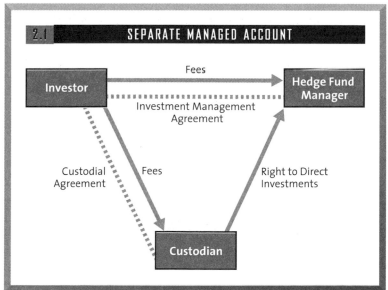

2.1 SEPARATE MANAGED ACCOUNT

investor usually must pay fees to the custodian in addition to the fees that he or she pays to the hedge fund manager. Compared with the structure of an existing fund, a managed account offers more flexibility, the ability to negotiate the manager's fees, customized risk management, and more transparency.

CHOOSING AN INVESTMENT VEHICLE

FOR MANY INVESTORS, existing vehicles are the only option because of the high minimum contribution that fund managers require to establish a managed account. Both investment vehicles have pros and cons that the investor should carefully consider in conjunction with his or her overall portfolio objectives before proceeding with an investment with a particular fund manager. For example, existing funds offer limited liability, no or low organizational costs, and a lower minimum required investment. However, funds generally have limited liquidity and delayed and limited position and performance reporting, and they offer no control over investment structure and terms, such as fees and brokerage arrangements. Alternatively, a managed account offers flexibility in structure and

2.2 EXISTING FUND VERSUS MANAGED ACCOUNT		
FORM OF INVESTMENT	PROS	CONS
EXISTING FUND	◆ Limited liability ◆ No upfront organizational costs ◆ Lower minimum investment	◆ Less liquidity ◆ No control over structure and terms
MANAGED ACCOUNT	◆ Immediate knowledge of managers' positions ◆ Negotiated structure and terms ◆ Higher liquidity	◆ Organizational costs ◆ Higher minimum investment ◆ No liability limitation

investment terms, a high level of liquidity, and high level of position and performance reporting. However, managed accounts involve higher organizational costs and unlimited liability and require a larger minimum investment. The pros and cons of existing funds and managed accounts are summarized in the table at left.

FUND OF FUNDS

ONE FURTHER METHOD for accessing hedge fund managers is worth noting here: the fund of funds. Like most domestic hedge funds, fund of funds are organized as limited partnerships with a general partner who receives a management fee from the limited partners (sometimes the general partner will also receive a performance fee). Unlike domestic hedge funds, they do not make direct investments. The manager of a fund of funds pools capital from investors and then allocates it to two or more hedge fund managers. The principle is similar to that of a mutual fund but on a larger scale. In a mutual fund, investors gain exposure to a pool of multiple securities that they otherwise could not afford. By making a single investment in a fund of funds, investors obtain access to a number of different hedge funds in which, because of the high minimum investment required by each, they could not invest individually. This approach permits them to diversify across instruments, strategies, and markets. It is a method

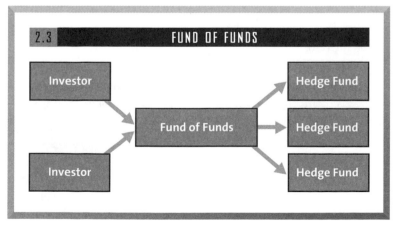

2.3 FUND OF FUNDS

for investors to gain exposure to a diversified batch of hedge funds without incurring the high administrative and research costs that would result if they invested in the funds individually. The cost of this diversified exposure is an extra layer of fees: on top of each hedge fund manager's management and performance fees, the fund of funds manager charges a similar management fee and sometimes a performance fee as well.

FEATURES OF
HEDGE FUND STRUCTURES

LEGAL FORM

HEDGE FUNDS COME in a variety of legal forms depending on where they are located and the type of investor that the fund organizer wishes to attract. To avoid entity-level tax, in the United States they are usually formed as limited partnerships or, in rare cases, limited liability companies or trusts. Limited partnerships are organized under state law (e.g., an Illinois limited partnership). The general form is not unique to hedge funds but rather is used for various businesses. A limited partnership has one or more general partners and a number of limited partners. The general partner can be an individual or a corporation, is responsible for the management and operation of the partnership, and has unlimited liability. The manager will typically be the general partner but acts through an entity to avoid unlimited personal liability for fund obligations. The general partner is responsible for the overhead expenses of running the fund (e.g., salaries, rent, telephone charges). In the past, if the general partner was a registered investment adviser (RIA), the fund could not charge a performance fee for a period of less than one year. Many existing hedge funds were constructed with this restriction in mind. However, as of July 1998 the SEC has dropped its twelve-month measurement period requirement for incentive fees. Thus, RIAs can now have monthly, quarterly, or semiannual incentive fees. More hedge fund managers are now registering as RIAs, which in turn will allow them to manage money in mutual funds. This also increases the percentage of hedge funds under a higher level of regulatory oversight. Although there are still other hurdles, I expect SEC regulations to be relaxed further so that many hedge fund strategies can be incorporated into traditional investment structures.

The limited partners have liability "limited" to the amount that they invest or "pay" for their limited partnership interests. Generally, they are allocated pro rata their share of all investments and expenses of the fund. However, sometimes funds provide that investors who enter after the initial closing do not participate in investments made before their admission date. This is particularly likely to be the case if the fund has illiquid, hard-to-value positions. Limited partners have a defined set of rights, as set forth in the limited partnership agreement. The limited partnership interests are not traded and cannot be sold to any other prospective investor. They can only be sold back to the partnership or "redeemed" under the procedures established in the agreement.

Offshore funds are funds organized outside the United States, usually in an offshore tax haven such as the Cayman Islands, Bermuda, the British Virgin Islands, the Bahamas, or Ireland. Typically, a corporate structure is used, but because of the tax haven, no entity-level tax is imposed. Instead of a general partner, these structures have a management company. Investors purchase shares. As is the case with domestic funds, their liability is limited to the amount that they invest. For tax reasons, offshore funds typically are composed primarily of non-U.S. investors. However, many managers of offshore funds permit tax-exempt U.S. investors to participate. Sometimes, fund managers will create both a domestic fund and a parallel offshore fund. In that case, the manager may offer one or both options to tax-exempt investors. (Sometimes, the manager will prefer to keep all tax-exempt investors in the offshore fund to avoid using up "slots" or to avoid the need

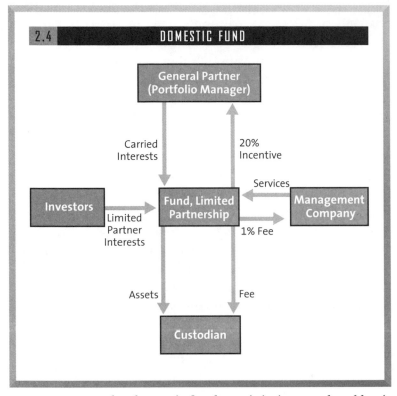

to structure the domestic fund to minimize unrelated business taxable income [UBTI].) Because the manager will receive a share of the profits earned on the client's investment, managers may prefer to create a domestic fund in which they act as the general partner so that they can receive their share as an allocation of capital gains or can defer recognition of gain until the underlying investments are sold. Alternatively, managers may wish to use an offshore fund structure so that they can defer receipt of fees for income tax purposes.

DOCUMENTATION

THREE MAIN DOCUMENTS involved in investing in hedge funds organized as limited partnerships are the offering memorandum, the limited partnership agreement, and the subscription agreement. Offshore hedge funds usually offer shares, so their documents will not include a limited

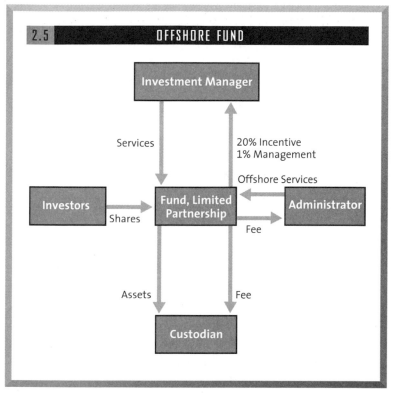

partnership agreement. The offering memorandum for offshore funds usually contains less disclosure than that for onshore funds.

OFFERING MEMORANDUM

THE OFFERING MEMORANDUM may also be called the private placement memorandum, disclosure document, prospectus, or any of a number of other variations. It provides a general discussion of the securities that the hedge fund is selling, a summary of the limited partnership agreement, fee structures, redemption provisions, background information on the manager and key personnel, a discussion of risks and conflicts of interest and taxation, and other information essential to making an investment decision.

LIMITED PARTNERSHIP AGREEMENT

THE LIMITED PARTNERSHIP agreement is the contract that the investor enters into as a limited partner to the partnership. It specifies the rights and obligation of the limited and general partners and how the partnership will be operated. As the partnership is organized under a state act, specific law that applies to the limited partnership is not described in the agreement.

SUBSCRIPTION AGREEMENT

THE SUBSCRIPTION AGREEMENT is an application for acceptance as a limited partner that includes investor information and representations of the investor's suitability for inclusion in the partnership. It is a signed offer to invest accompanied by a check or wire transfer of the investment amount. If it is accepted by the general partner, then the assets are placed in the fund and the investor becomes a limited partner and investor. Usually, the only further evidence of the transaction is a letter from the manager to the investor confirming that the investor was accepted.

REGISTRATION AND REGULATION—THE PRIVATE NATURE OF HEDGE FUNDS

HEDGE FUNDS ARE usually private investment vehicles. In the United States, this means that, under one of the available exemptions, the securities offered to investors (the limited partnership interests) are not registered with the SEC for offer to the public. The exemptions specify certain conditions that must be complied with to avoid registration. These generally deal with the types of investors allowed to invest in the fund, how many can invest, and how the investors can be solicited. Until 1997, the 3(c)(1) exemption limited participants to ninety-nine accredited investors. An accredited investor is **1** an individual who has made $200,000 a year in income for the past two years and has a reasonable expectation of doing so in the future; **2** one who, together with a spouse, has an income of

$300,000 per year; or **3** one who has a net worth of $1 million, excluding home and automobile. A 3(c)(1) fund cannot offer securities publicly.

In 1997, under the National Securities Markets Improvements Act, a second exemption, 3(c)(7), was enacted to create a new exclusion from the definition of an investment company for investment pools if all its investors are qualified purchasers. A qualified purchaser is **1** an individual holding at least $5 million in investments; **2** a family company that owns not less than $5 million in investments; **3** a person, acting for his or her own account or for the accounts of other qualified purchasers, who owns and invests on a discretionary basis at least $25 million in investments; or **4** a company (regardless of the amount of such company's investments) if each beneficial owner of the company's securities is a qualified purchaser. Both exemptions require material information to be disclosed.

Hedge fund managers are investment advisers. Many are also exempt from registration with the SEC because they have a limited number of investors and do not advertise themselves as investment advisers. A growing number of hedge fund managers, however, are registering in response to investor and business demands.

FEES AND EXPENSES

HEDGE FUNDS CHARGE two fees: a management fee and an incentive fee. The management fee is based on a percentage of the assets in the fund, usually 1 or 2 percent each year. It is paid monthly or quarterly and may be due at the beginning or end of each period. The fee is automatically deducted pro rata from each investor's account. The incentive fee or "carried interest" is the hedge fund manager's share in the fund's profits. Usually this is 20 percent and is paid annually in the United States, but it may be calculated monthly or quarterly offshore. Two terms should be noted when reviewing incentive fees: hurdle rate and high water mark. A hurdle is the return that must be earned each year before the manager starts participating in the profits. Often, the Treasury bill rate is used. Use of a high water mark requires a manager to attain performance above the highest previous level before earning additional incentive fees. In other words, the investor does not pay for covering the same ground twice because losses must be made up before the manager begins participating in profits. Most hedge funds have high water marks but not hurdles. Specifics on how fees are calculated are described in the offering materials and fund documentation.

The fund also pays legal, audit, administrative, and other expenses, all of which should be described in the fund documentation.

INVESTMENT SIZE

THE MINIMUM INVESTMENT size for hedge funds ranges from $100,000 to $10 million but usually is in the $500,000 to $1 million range. Minimums are usually larger onshore because regulations limit the number of investors. In the early stages, when a hedge fund has few investors and is trying to raise funds, it normally offers lower minimums and more flexibility to waive the minimum and accept a lesser amount. As the number of investors in the fund increases, the remaining slots become more valuable, and managers are less likely to waive the minimum. In many cases, the fund actually raises the minimum for new investors and in some cases kicks out the smaller players to make room for larger allocations.

Because of the more limited asset capacity of many of the hedge fund strategies, many managers also limit the size of any one investor to ensure a diversified client base. Funds that do not wish to become subject to ERISA restrictions cannot have more than 25 percent ERISA assets.

LOCKUP PERIODS

A LOCKUP PERIOD is the length of time that investors must remain invested before their investment can be redeemed or becomes subject to the standard liquidity provision. The lockup period for hedge funds ranges from six months to five years, but the lockup in U.S. funds is usually one year. It works like this: if the lockup is one year, then an investor who invests on January 1 cannot redeem until December 31 of the same year. Continuing this example, if liquidity is quarterly, the next date on which a redemption would be allowed would be March 31 of the following year.

LIQUIDITY

IN A HEDGE FUND context, most people refer to the time periods for which investors may redeem their investment and have their money returned from the fund as liquidity. For example, quarterly liquidity indicates an investor can get out at the end of each calendar quarter, whereas monthly liquidity permits investor redemption at the end of each month. One mistake many first-time investors make is not factoring in the notice period that they are required to observe before they can redeem their investments. Unlike mutual funds or publicly traded securities, hedge funds cannot generate cash for investor redemption on short notice and require a notice period that ranges from thirty to ninety days. For example, for a fund that allows redemption at the end of each calendar quarter and requires a sixty-day notice, an investor wishing to redeem on June 30 must notify the fund in writing by April 30. If the investor waits until May 7 to notify the fund, he or she cannot get out until September 30. The redemption provisions also specify within what time frame a fund must actually pay the investor back in full. In the above example, the fund might have thirty days to pay 90 percent of the investment. The remaining 10 percent is held back until the fund's year-end audit is completed, which may mean that final payment will be received by the investor in March or April of the following year. This holdover provision generally only applies to investors who redeem the full amount of their investment.

Hedge funds need not make payment in cash. For certain funds generally, and for many funds under extreme circumstances such as liquidation, payment can be made in securities rather than in cash. In particular, this is the case for funds holding private or illiquid securities, such as those of bankrupt companies. However, it is not the case for all hedge funds, and some hedge fund managers make every effort to accommodate investors by returning their capital as early as possible and in cash. A fund's offering memorandum will specify its ability to make payments in cash or securities.

PERFORMANCE AND REPORTING

ALMOST ALL HEDGE FUNDS do not calculate performance or changes in NAV on a daily basis like mutual funds but rather make estimates on a monthly basis (some equity market neutral funds dealing in easily priced securities now provide daily NAVs). Some still only report quarterly and others put out weekly estimates, but the industry as a whole is on a monthly estimated performance basis. There is no standard reporting format, with some hedge funds providing quarterly faxes of percentage profit or loss and others sending out detailed monthly statements to each investor with a letter describing the fund's investment activities and results. Most managers, however, provide monthly return estimates for the prior month within two weeks by fax, mail, or E-mail. Audits are conducted annually for almost all funds and provided to investors with tax reporting documentation such as for K1s (partnership tax forms).

TAX ISSUES

THE TAX CONSEQUENCES incurred by a hedge fund vary widely from strategy to strategy and for each manager's approach within each strategy. The impact varies from structure to structure as well, so investors should consult experts to determine the tax implications of a specific fund. Some general comments can be made here. As mentioned earlier, most U.S.-based hedge funds are organized as limited partnerships that allow tax consequences to pass through to the investor. This means that tax-related activities such as profits, losses (long-term and short-term), and consequences of leverage to tax-exempt institutions such as UBTI (unrelated business taxable income) will figure into each investor's tax calculation. Investment programs can generate UBTI if **1** they use leverage or **2** they involve receipt of trade or business income, such as advisory or breakup fees.Some tax-exempt investors are unwilling to tolerate any UBTI. Others will accept UBTI provided that the net return is sufficiently high to offset the tax consequences.

Assuming that the fund is structured as a corporation rather than a pass-through entity such as a partnership, pass-through trust, or limited liability company, an offshore corporation is generally considered to cut off tax consequences by delivering profit or loss through the appreciation or depreciation of the shares purchased by the investor. Therefore, offshore funds are often offered so that tax-exempt investors may invest in leveraged programs. Taxable investors do not care about UBTI. Therefore, if a domestic fund includes both taxable and nontaxable investors, there is a conflict of interest as to whether the manager considers investments based on pre-UBTI or post-UBTI returns. Managed accounts and offshore funds avoid this issue. In general, tax-exempt investors are not otherwise concerned about the level of taxable income generated by a fund for its taxable investors. However, both taxable and tax-exempt investors aim to avoid funds that pay tax at the entity level and need to consider liability for taxes in foreign jurisdictions. Sometimes, taxable investors are able to receive tax credits for withholding taxes paid to other jurisdictions that are not available to tax-exempt investors. Another tax impact worth noting here is that offshore funds have withholding obligations on dividends that may range from a few basis points ($\frac{1}{100}$ of a percentage point) to a few percent, depending on the investment strategy. It is one of the reasons (slightly higher fees offshore being another) that the performance of offshore funds tends to underperform onshore "sister" funds.

ERISA CONSIDERATIONS

ERISA DIRECTLY AFFECTS the pension policies of corporations and unions. If benefit plan investors constitute less than 25 percent of the aggregate commitments to a hedge fund, the fund is not deemed to hold plan assets and is not subject to ERISA restrictions on transactions with prohibited persons nor to ERISA fee limits. Additionally, the plan fiduciary does not have liability with respect to the disposition of those assets by the fund (although the fiduciary may be held liable with respect to the decision to place the assets in the fund). If a managed account structure is used by an ERISA plan, the account will constitute plan assets. For liability reasons, ERISA plans often insist on investing only with RIAs or, if a manager is not registered with the SEC, using an RIA to recommend making the investment. Depending on the investment strategy (e.g., investments in derivatives), it may be necessary for the manager to qualify as a qualified professional asset manager, which, among other things, requires that the manager have at least $50 million in assets under management and $750,000 in equity, and that no pension plan can constitute 20 percent of the manager's assets under management. Some ERISA investors create in-house asset managers to facilitate the making of investments in unregistered entities without incurring the expense of an independent adviser. The in-house asset manager is registered as an investment adviser. As a result of recent amendments to securities laws, it generally is no longer possible for a manager to register as an investment adviser under federal law unless the adviser has at least $25 million under discretionary management. Advisers controlling smaller amounts will usually register with the states. For a limited time, state-registered investment advisers provide the same level of protection to the ERISA fiduciary as do federally registered advisers.

INVESTING
With Knowledge

PART

I

CHAPTER

Hedge Fund
STRATEGIES

BROAD RANGE OF strategies are operated under the hedge fund structure. This spectrum includes non-leveraged hedged styles and highly leveraged directional approaches.[4]

To comprehend these strategies, an investor must understand the different elements of investing that make up these strategies. This knowledge builds a framework from which to compare the different approaches. Although some elements are not vastly different from those that constitute traditional investing methods, others are unique to hedge fund strategies. This chapter discusses five important groups of elements: tools and techniques, instruments and markets, performance, sources of return, and measures for controlling risk.

TOOLS AND TECHNIQUES

LEVERAGE

WHEN INVESTORS BORROW funds to increase the amount that they have invested in a particular position, they are using leverage. Investors use leverage when they believe that the return from the position will exceed the cost of the borrowed funds. Investors who use leverage increase the risk of their investment; therefore, they usually try to use it only in extremely low-risk situations that can benefit from low-cost funding. Sometimes, managers use leverage to enable them to put on new, favorable positions without having to take off other positions prematurely. Managers who target very small price discrepancies or spreads will often use leverage to magnify the returns from these discrepancies.

SHORT SELLING

SHORT SELLING IS selling a security that the manager does not own. The security is borrowed from a bank, an insurance company, or a major brokerage firm that holds securities for its customers. To borrow the security, the fund manager needs some form of collateral, such as other equities or U.S. Treasury bills (T bills). After borrowing the security, the manager immediately sells it on the open market with the intention of buying it back later at a lower price and returning it to the lender. Until that future date, the proceeds from the short sale earn interest in a money market account. If the price of the security sold short declines, then the short seller will realize profits equal to the difference between the price at which he or she sold the security and the price at which he or she buys it back. Alternatively, if the price of the security sold short appreciates, then the manager will realize losses equal to the difference between the price at which he or she must buy the security and the price at which he or she sold it.

Different strategies use short selling in different fashions. Some use it as a trading technique from which to derive profits, and others use it as a hedge against market declines. Managers must always consider whether a security is available to sell short. The securities of larger, more liquid companies tend to be more readily available to sell short than those of smaller, less liquid entities.

HEDGING

HEDGING IS TAKING a secondary position with the expressed purpose of counterbalancing a known risk involved with a primary position. This can be accomplished by taking positions in specifically related securities for specific risks or by purchasing index options for market risks. These positions are taken to offset changes in economic conditions other than the core investment idea, such as a change in the overall level of stock market prices, a change in interest rates, or a change in foreign exchange rates. The basic hedging technique is to purchase a primary long position and a secondary short position in a similar security to offset the effect that any changes in the overall level of the financial market or sector will have on the long position. For example, if an investor's rationale for buying a bond is that he or she thinks that the market has mispriced the credit risk of the issuing company, he or she would hedge against interest rate changes by buying a long position in the bond and a short position in a similar bond. If interest rates change, then any adverse effect on the long position will be offset by a positive effect on the short position. The process is reversed if a manager is trying to hedge against price increases. Alternatively, a manager can purchase index options to hedge movements in overall price levels. Hedging is a way in which an investor can neutralize the effects of systemic changes in market conditions.

ARBITRAGE

ARBITRAGE IS THE simultaneous purchase and sale of a related or similar security to profit from a pricing discrepancy—for example, purchasing an undervalued convertible bond (a bond convertible into common stock) and selling short the underlying common stock.

INVESTMENT INSTRUMENTS AND MARKETS

INSTRUMENTS

THE ASSETS THAT are available for purchase in financial markets are called investment instruments. These include stocks and bonds and all levels of financial derivatives. Derivatives are securities whose value is based on or is derived from the value of another instrument. For instance, the value of derivatives such as futures and options is based on the future value of a stock market index or the future value of Eurodollar deposits.

One way to distinguish different investment strategies is

by the instruments in which they invest. Many hedge fund strategies invest in instruments avoided by traditional investment funds, such as futures; options; asset-backed securities; or the bonds, bank debt, or trade claims of companies with low credit ratings or in bankruptcy proceedings.

MARKETS

A MARKET CAN refer to geography or asset classes. The grouping can be based on criteria such as an asset or instrument type (e.g., the stock market or the futures market), or on geographic location (e.g., Asian emerging market or Russian market). The term can be confusing because it is used on many different levels, but at base it refers to a mechanism by which a group of investors and suppliers who are interested in a group of assets that share some underlying characteristic are brought together.

RISK CONTROL

RISK, QUITE SIMPLY, is exposure to uncertainty. There are two components to investment risk: uncertainty and exposure to that uncertainty. To control risk, managers must reduce uncertainty about future events or reduce the exposure of their portfolio to uncertainty about the future. Many of them will use hedging strategies (see above) to do so. Other common techniques follow.

RESEARCH

RESEARCH REFERS TO the gathering, analysis, interpretation, and interpolation of information. Since markets act on information, a manager who obtains better or earlier information, or superior interpretation of it, has an edge on the market. Good research allows managers to take positions in instruments that are mispriced, in an absolute or relative sense, before the market reacts. The most common techniques for identifying such securities are in-depth fundamental and technical analysis.

DIVERSIFICATION

DIVERSIFICATION IS THE creation of variations in a portfolio through positions to reduce the adverse impact of a loss in any one position. Investment managers diversify their holdings to reduce exposure to risks associated with any one position, industry, sector, or type of instrument.

The logic of diversification can be implemented on many levels. Investment managers will diversify their holdings across industries, sectors, instruments, time horizons, and even investment styles.

POSITION LIMITS

MANY INVESTMENT MANAGERS limit the size of positions in their portfolios to restrain the damage that any individual position can have on their portfolios. Position size may be based on a percentage of assets or on a specified maximum loss on each position. This ensures a certain level of diversification.

BUY/SELL TARGETS

MANY INVESTMENT MANAGERS perform their analyses relative to a market and estimate the value at which they think a security in which they have a position should be trading. Once it reaches that estimate, they liquidate the position because they believe the profit opportunity has run its course. Targets quantitatively articulate the investment disciplines imposed by the manager.

STOP-LOSS LIMITS

MANY INVESTMENT MANAGERS will not keep a security in their portfolio if it declines past a predetermined point. A stop-loss limit identifies the maximum loss a manager is willing to take on a position.

PERFORMANCE

THE PERFORMANCE OF hedge fund strategies is often presented and evaluated in terms of absolute return and risk-adjusted return. Unlike traditional investments that can be compared to, or benchmarked against, market indices, most hedge fund strategies are not directly related to the direction of a specific market and therefore cannot be evaluated in that manner.

Increasingly their performance is compared to indices representing managers pursuing the same or a similar strategy.

HEDGE FUND STRATEGIES

THE FOLLOWING PARAGRAPHS summarize the eleven hedge fund strategies covered in this book. In addition, this chapter includes charts that show how the amount of assets each strategy controls has changed in the 1990s in relation to the average annual returns of those funds. These graphs allow readers to note the relationships between assets controlled and fund performance. As might be expected, more funds usually mean more assets. However, this is by no means a one-to-one relationship.

For example, there are presently more event-driven funds than there are macro funds, but the macro funds control about three times as many assets. When a strategy is producing high returns, not only are there ample investment profits that are increasing assets, but allocations from new investors will increase assets as well. New funds will be created to share in the profits and attract some of the new allocations. When the amount of assets allocated to a strategy increases, it is usually some combination of these factors. The process is reversed when a strategy is producing poor results.

FIXED-INCOME ARBITRAGE

FIXED-INCOME ARBITRAGE specialists take offsetting long and short positions in related fixed-income securities and their derivatives whose values are mathematically or historically interrelated but in which the arbitrageurs believe that the relationship is temporarily dislocated or will soon change. They realize a profit when the skewed relationship between the securities returns to its expected range or shifts in the manner that the arbitrageur anticipated. The differences between these related instruments are usually slight; therefore the arbitrageur uses leverage to magnify the small changes in the relationship between the instruments. The arbitrageur usually neutralizes the position's exposure to interest rate changes to some extent by taking offsetting long and short positions, so the risk level is less than it appears to be given the amount of leverage used.

Figure 3.1 shows how the returns and total assets of fixed-income arbitrage funds have changed thus far in the 1990s. The amount of assets under management

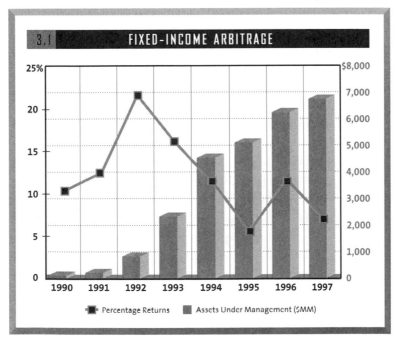

3.1 FIXED-INCOME ARBITRAGE

Percentage Returns   Assets Under Management ($MM)

grew as the number of fixed-income arbitrage funds grew. From year-end 1994 to year-end 1995, the amount of assets under management flattened a bit. This was to be expected because fixed-income arbitrage funds had their worst year, performance-wise, in 1995, with about 6 percent returns. Not surprisingly, assets increased rapidly between 1992 and 1994, with fixed-income arbitrageurs registering their highest returns in 1992 and 1993.

EQUITY MARKET-NEUTRAL (STATISTICAL ARBITRAGE)

EQUITY-MARKET-NEUTRAL strategists construct portfolios that consist of approximately equal dollar amounts of offsetting long and short equity positions. They use sophisticated quantitative and qualitative models to select stocks. Stocks expected to outperform the market are held long, and stocks expected to underperform the market are sold short. By balancing long and short positions, market-neutral strategists insulate their portfolios from any systemic turn of events that affects valuations of the stock market as a whole. Such investors often apply the same logic across sectors, industries, and investment styles. Thus, market-neutral strategists ensure that their profits are derived from the ability of their models to pick over- and undervalued stocks, regardless of market direction.

Figure 3.2 shows how the returns and total assets of equity-market-neutral funds changed in the course of the 1990s. The most interesting thing to note is the sharp increase in assets under management from year-end 1996 to year-end 1997. Although equity-market-neutral funds performed well during this period, much of this increase must be attributed to new allocations. It may be that investors who are wary of the long bull market are putting some of their money into conservative market-neutral funds that provide good downside protection.

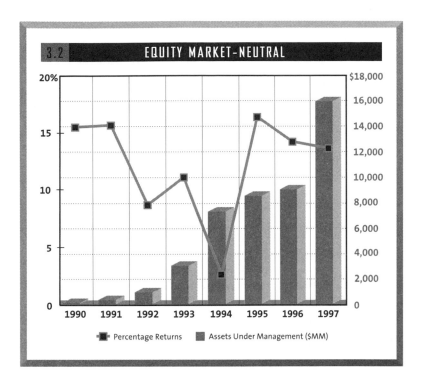

3.2   **EQUITY MARKET-NEUTRAL**

■ Percentage Returns   ■ Assets Under Management ($MM)

CONVERTIBLE ARBITRAGE

CONVERTIBLE ARBITRAGEURS construct long portfolios of convertible bonds and hedge these positions by selling short the underlying stock of each bond. Convertible bonds are bonds that can be converted into a fixed number of shares of the issuing company's stock. Convertible bonds are hybrid securities that have features of both a bond and a stock, and therefore their valuations reflect both types of instruments. Generally, the price of the convertible will decline less rapidly than that of the underlying stock in a falling equity market and will mirror the price of the stock more closely in a rising equity market. Convertible arbitrageurs extract arbitrage profits from these complex pricing relationships by purchasing the convertible bond and selling short its underlying stock.

Figure 3.3 on the following page shows how the returns and total assets of convertible arbitrage funds changed in the course of the 1990s. Negative returns in 1994

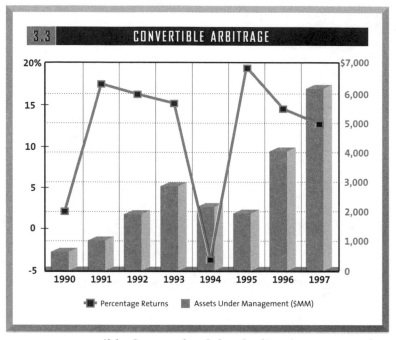

3.3   CONVERTIBLE ARBITRAGE

Percentage Returns   Assets Under Management ($MM)

are responsible for much of the decline in assets under management from year-end 1993 to year-end 1995. Excellent returns from 1995 onward have driven the sharp increase in funds under management and led to new allocations. It is interesting that the number of convertible arbitrage funds is leveling off. Because there are limited numbers of convertible issues, this strategy is not capable of supporting a very large number of funds.

MERGER (RISK) ARBITRAGE

RISK OR MERGER arbitrage specialists invest in companies that are being acquired or are involved in a merger. Typically, they will buy the common stock of a company being acquired or merging with another company and sell short the stock of the acquiring company. The target company's stock will usually trade at a discount to the value that it will attain after the merger is completed because all mergers take time and involve some risk that the transaction will not occur. If the transaction fails to be completed, then the price of the target company's stock usually declines.

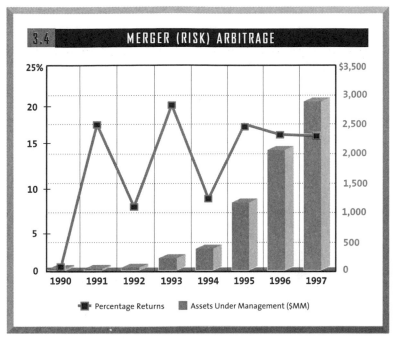

3.4 MERGER (RISK) ARBITRAGE

Risk arbitrage specialists make profits when they correctly anticipate the outcome of an announced merger and capture the spread between the current market price of the target company's stock and the price to which it will appreciate if the deal is completed.

Figure 3.4 shows how the returns and total assets of merger arbitrage funds changed in the course of the 1990s. Assets under management have grown steadily since year-end 1994, reflecting the excellent returns that have resulted from increased merger activity. The still relatively low number of funds using the merger arbitrage strategy reflects the limited number of good merger arbitrage situations.

DISTRESSED SECURITIES

DISTRESSED SECURITIES specialists invest in the securities of companies that are experiencing financial or operational difficulties. Distressed situations include reorganizations, bankruptcies, distressed sales, and other corporate restructurings. The pricing of these securities is often dis-

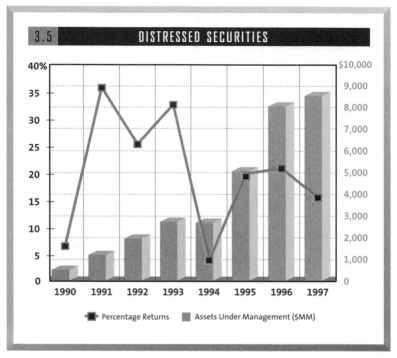

3.5   DISTRESSED SECURITIES

Percentage Returns   Assets Under Management ($MM)

torted because many traditional buyers either legally or customarily must sell the securities of troubled companies. Therefore, a pricing discount occurs that reflects both these structural anomalies and uncertainty about the outcome of the event. Depending on the manager's style, he or she may invest in bank debt, corporate debt, trade claims, common stock, or warrants. Distressed securities specialists make profits when they correctly anticipate the value that a distressed enterprise will obtain following reorganization.

Figure 3.5 shows how the returns and total assets of distressed securities funds changed in the course of the 1990s. The slight decline in assets under management between year-end 1993 and year-end 1994 corresponds to the low returns that distressed funds registered in 1994. The rapid growth since then reflects the strategy's solid performance from 1995 to 1997.

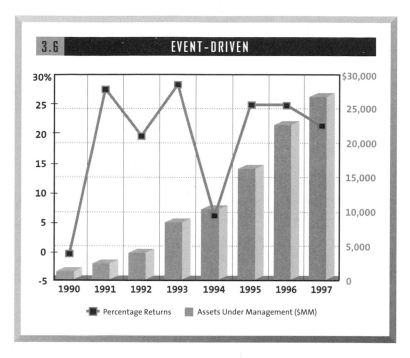

3.6 EVENT-DRIVEN

Percentage Returns   Assets Under Management ($MM)

EVENT-DRIVEN STRATEGIES

PRACTITIONERS OF event-driven investment strategies invest in the outcomes of the significant events that occur during corporate life cycles, such as bankruptcies, financial restructurings, mergers, acquisitions, and the spin-off of a division or subsidiary. The uncertainty about the outcome of these events creates investment opportunities for a specialist who can correctly anticipate their outcomes. Generally, these extraordinary corporate events fall into three categories: risk arbitrage opportunities, distressed securities situations, and special situations. Event-driven specialists will shift the majority weighting of their portfolios to reflect the corporate events that offer the best investment opportunities.

Figure 3.6 shows how the returns and total assets of event-driven funds changed in the course of the 1990s. The steady growth in both the number of event-driven funds and the total assets under management reflects the very strong performance and relatively low volatility of this strategy from 1991 onward. The only exception, 1994, is responsible for the slight flattening between year-end 1993 and year-end 1994.

MACRO INVESTING

MACRO INVESTORS MAKE profits by identifying extreme price-value disparities and persistent trends in stock markets, interest rates, foreign exchange rates, and physical commodities and making leveraged bets on the price movements that they anticipate in these markets. To identify these extreme pricing disparities, they use a top-down global approach that concentrates on forecasting how global macroeconomic and political events affect the valuations of financial instruments. They have the broadest investment mandate of any of the hedge fund strategies, with the ability to hold positions in practically any market with any instrument. Macro investors make profits by correctly anticipating price movements in global markets and having the flexibility to use any investment approach that allows them to take advantage of extreme price dislocations that they identify. They may use a focused approach or diversify across approaches. Often they will pursue a number of other hedge fund strategies in addition to making leveraged directional bets.

Figure 3.7 shows how the returns and total assets of macro funds changed in the course of the 1990s. The large amount of assets controlled by relatively few funds is characteristic of macro strategies. The large jump in assets under management from 1991 to 1993 corresponds to outstanding performance, including returns in excess of 50 percent in 1993. This was the period when George Soros became famous for making more than a billion dollars on changes in the pound sterling. This period of rapid growth was followed by negative returns in 1994. As a result, assets under management shrank in 1994, but the further shrinkage in 1995 and 1996 cannot be attributed to performance alone. Although macro funds still

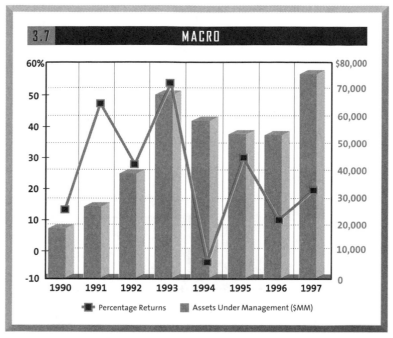

3.7 MACRO

Percentage Returns ■ Assets Under Management ($MM)

control 20 percent of total hedge fund assets, this figure is down from 50 percent in 1990.

SECTOR

SECTOR SPECIALISTS INVEST in a group of companies or segment of the economy with a common product or market. They can invest long and short in various instruments and diversify their portfolios across either the entire sector or some subsector. The managers of sector funds combine fundamental financial analysis with industry expertise to identify the best profit opportunities in the sector. The opportunities that they identify are not necessarily growth stocks; in a down market, they may make profits by identifying the worst-performing stocks in the sector. They will sometimes hedge against market or sector price declines by buying index put options or selling short overvalued stocks.

Figure 3.8 on the following page shows how the returns and total assets of sector funds changed in the course of the 1990s. The number of sector funds and the

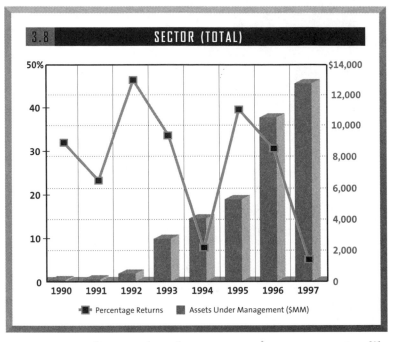

3.8   **SECTOR (TOTAL)**

Percentage Returns   Assets Under Management ($MM)

amount of assets that they manage have grown steadily to reflect the huge returns that they produced in all but 1994 and 1997. Predictably, asset growth slowed in both of those years.

EQUITY HEDGE

EQUITY HEDGE STRATEGISTS combine core long holdings of equities with short sales of stock or stock index options. Their portfolios may be anywhere from net long to net short, depending on market conditions. They increase long exposure in bull markets and decrease it or even go net short in a bear market. Generally, the short exposure is intended to generate an ongoing positive return in addition to acting as a hedge against a general stock market decline. In a rising market, equity hedge strategists expect their long holdings to appreciate more than the market and their short holdings to appreciate less than the market. Similarly, in a declining market, they expect their short holdings to fall more rapidly than the market falls and their long holdings to fall less rapidly than

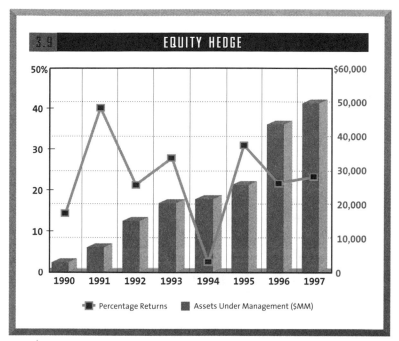

3.9 EQUITY HEDGE

Percentage Returns ■ Assets Under Management ($MM)

the market. The idea is to take long positions in stocks that will outperform the market and sell short stocks that will underperform the market. Equity hedge fund managers' source of return is similar to that of traditional stock pickers on the upside, but they use short selling and hedging to outperform the market on the downside.

Equity nonhedge strategists use a strategy that is similar to traditional long-only strategies but with the freedom to use varying amounts of leverage. Although most of them reserve the right to sell short, short sales are not an ongoing component of their investment portfolios, and many have not carried short positions at all. Equity nonhedge is treated as a variation of the equity hedge strategy. At heart, these are both concentrated stock-picking strategies, one that hedges market risk by augmenting core long positions with short positions and the other that forgoes that short exposure. The freedom to use leverage, take short positions, and hedge long positions is a strategic advantage that differentiates equity hedge strategists from traditional long-only equity investors.

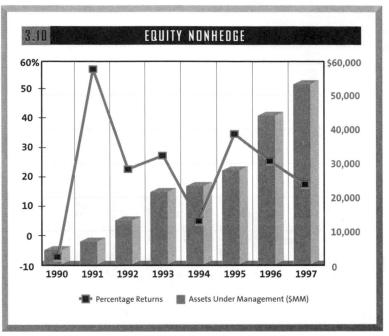

Figure 3.9 on the previous page and Figure 3.10 above show how the returns and total assets of equity hedge and equity nonhedge funds changed in the course of the 1990s. Equity hedge funds have grown steadily both in number and assets, with strong performance in all but 1994. Not surprisingly, equity nonhedge funds have followed a similar path in the bull market of the 1990s. Nearly a third of all hedge funds are presently using primarily one of these two strategies.

EMERGING MARKETS

EMERGING MARKETS SPECIALISTS make primarily long investments in the securities of companies in countries with developing or "emerging" financial markets. They use specialized knowledge and an on-the-ground presence in markets in which financial information is often scarce to create an informational advantage that allows them to take advantage of mispricings caused by emerging market inefficiencies. They make profits by mining these markets for undervalued assets and pur-

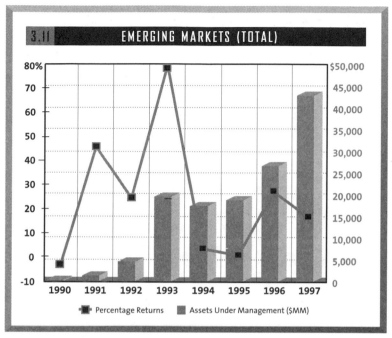

3.11 EMERGING MARKETS (TOTAL)

Percentage Returns ■ Assets Under Management ($MM)

chasing them before the market corrects itself.

Figure 3.11 shows how the returns and total assets of emerging market funds changed in the course of the 1990s. The number of such funds has grown from just a handful in 1990 to more than 350 at year-end 1997, reflecting the ever-increasing interest of managers and investors alike in the opportunities offered by newly created markets. Assets under management quadrupled in 1993, when emerging market funds produced nearly 80 percent returns. Poor performance in 1994 and 1995 restrained asset growth, but it rebounded in 1996 and 1997 when returns again were strong. These trends are aggregate of the different emerging markets, each of which had its own ups and downs in this period. However, it is beyond the scope of this book to discuss in detail the emerging markets in eastern Europe, Latin America, and Asia separately.

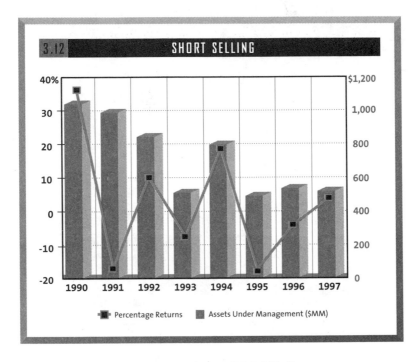

SHORT SELLING

A SHORT SELLING strategy seeks to profit from a decline in the value of stocks. It involves selling a security that the investor does not own to take advantage of an anticipated price decline. The short seller borrows the securities from a third party to deliver them to the purchaser. The short seller eventually repurchases the securities on the open market to return them to the third-party lender. If the short seller can repurchase the stock at a lower price than what he or she sold it for, then he or she makes a profit. In addition, the short seller earns interest on the cash proceeds from the short sale of stock. However, if the price of the stock rises, then he or she incurs a loss. Generally, a short seller must pledge other securities or cash equal to the market price of the borrowed securities with the lender.

Figure 3.12 shows how the returns and total assets of short selling funds changed in the course of the 1990s. The number of short selling funds had been low throughout the 1990s and topped out in 1994 when they produced good returns. This is also reflected in assets under management, which grew in 1994, but fell in the losing years of 1991, 1993, and 1995 when short sellers recorded substantial losses. Although the number and assets of short sellers dwindled during much of the 1990s, this trend reversed in 1998 as more investors looked to position for an equity market decline.

UNIVERSE OF
HEDGE FUND STRATEGIES

HEDGE FUND MANAGERS sometimes speak of a universe of stocks or bonds that they consider for investment. The universe of hedge fund strategies described in this book will give investors insight into the majority of investment approaches practiced by hedge fund managers. Although some strategies have been omitted, the eleven covered in this book now account for about 90 percent of all hedge fund assets. To be fair to the hedge fund managers, each one has a unique approach. However, this book places the methodologies in categories, focusing on their similarities. Funds that do not fit formally into these categories are most likely using similar investing principles. In the future, new approaches will inevitably be created that combine elements of investing in ways not corresponding to the categories discussed here. In fact, new strategies are added every year. However, the universe of hedge fund strategies covered in this book gives investors a useful point of reference for considering present and future investment approaches used by hedge fund managers.

Figures 3.13 and 3.14 on the following two pages show the percentage of total hedge fund assets controlled by each of the strategies at the end of 1990 and again at the end of 1997. In both years, the selected strategies represented about 90 percent of all hedge fund assets, so neither graph is intended to add up to 100 percent. The graphs clearly illustrate the changes that have taken place in the industry. All the strategies except for short selling show growth in assets in the 1990s, but some grew

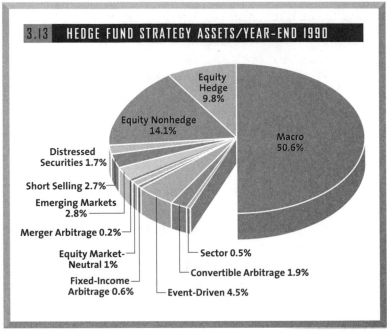

3.13 HEDGE FUND STRATEGY ASSETS/YEAR-END 1990

Equity Hedge 9.8%

Equity Nonhedge 14.1%

Distressed Securities 1.7%

Short Selling 2.7%

Emerging Markets 2.8%

Merger Arbitrage 0.2%

Equity Market-Neutral 1%

Fixed-Income Arbitrage 0.6%

Macro 50.6%

Sector 0.5%

Convertible Arbitrage 1.9%

Event-Driven 4.5%

faster than others. In addition, some strategies started with far fewer assets. For example, macro strategies have grown in assets but at the same time have lost overall market share, declining from half the assets in the industry to one-fifth. Niche and specialist strategies have gained ground as a percentage of overall industry assets. The biggest gainers have been sector funds, emerging market funds, equity-market-neutral funds, and event-driven funds. Equity hedge funds have also gained a larger share of the growing body of hedge fund assets during this bull market period. These changes cannot be attributed to any single factor, but reflect a trend toward more specialization and less aggressive returns. The strategy weightings will continue to change in response to the changing opportunities that the market offers and the shifting makeup of its investor base.

RISK/REWARD SPECTRUM

THE VARIOUS HEDGE FUND strategies have very different risk/reward characteristics and should be evaluated indi-

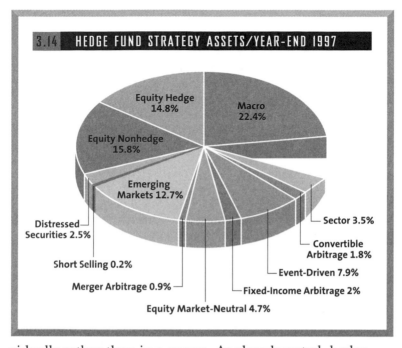

3.14 HEDGE FUND STRATEGY ASSETS/YEAR-END 1997

Equity Hedge 14.8%

Macro 22.4%

Equity Nonhedge 15.8%

Emerging Markets 12.7%

Distressed Securities 2.5%

Short Selling 0.2%

Merger Arbitrage 0.9%

Equity Market-Neutral 4.7%

Fixed-Income Arbitrage 2%

Event-Driven 7.9%

Convertible Arbitrage 1.8%

Sector 3.5%

vidually rather than in a group. As already noted, hedge funds are heterogeneous, which explains why it's important to categorize them by the core strategy that the fund manager uses. Some hedge fund strategies are aggressive in nature, such as macro funds. Others, such as nonleveraged market-neutral funds, are conservative. Many have significantly lower risk than a portfolio of long stocks and bonds for the same levels of return. Overall, hedge fund strategies, except for short selling, have performed well on a risk-adjusted basis at all points on the risk/reward spectrum. The graph on the following page plots the average annualized return of each strategy against its annualized standard deviation. The risk/reward profiles of T bills and the Standard and Poor's 500 index of blue-chip stocks provide a basis of comparison. The capital market line drawn through the T bills and the S&P 500 represents a rough estimate of the expected trade-off between risk and return for traditional investments. Notice that the risk/reward profile of every hedge fund strategy except short selling is above the line. In addition,

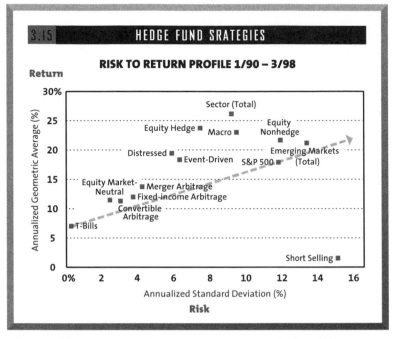

3.15   **HEDGE FUND SRATEGIES**

keep this spectrum in mind as you read the different strategy chapters. Think of how it reflects the market environment in the 1990s, and how it might change when market conditions shift.

Each of the strategy chapters discusses the core strategy principles, the investment process, the advantages and disadvantages of the strategy, and its performance in the 1990s. The short version of the strategy is reprinted at the beginning of each chapter to introduce the most important elements to look for in the chapter. For those readers looking strictly for numbers, the performance section includes month-by-month and summary statistics for each strategy. The most important concepts from the chapter are highlighted in the Summary Points section that follows the performance statistics. Finally, key words and concepts in bold type are defined in the Key Terms section at the end of each chapter.

CHAPTER

Fixed-Income
ARBITRAGE

FIXED-INCOME OR *relative value arbitrage specialists take offsetting long and short positions in related fixed-income securities and their derivatives whose values are mathematically or historically interrelated but in which the arbitrageur believes that the relationship is temporarily dislocated or will soon change. They realize a profit when the skewed relationship between the securities returns to its expected range or shifts in the manner that the arbitrageur anticipated. The differences between these related instruments are usually slight; therefore the arbitrageur uses leverage to magnify the small changes in the relationship between the instruments. The arbitrageur usually neutralizes the position's exposure to interest rate changes to some extent by taking offsetting long and short positions, so the risk level is less than it appears to be given the amount of leverage used.*

OVER TIME, NEW **FIXED-INCOME** instruments and their derivatives have evolved to meet suppliers' need and investors' demand for more diverse investment options. Consequently, the universe of fixed-income issues has expanded to tailor cash flows and modify various categories of risk to investors' preferences. It now includes everything from Treasury bills to corporate bonds to swaps to asset-backed securities. Even though they behave differently from more traditional fixed-income instruments under certain circumstances, when these newer instruments are mispriced they provide fixed-income arbitrageurs with the same kind of **ARBITRAGE** profit opportunities.

Because of the proliferation of fixed-income instruments, there are enough slight variations of the basic fixed-income arbitrage strategy to fill an entire book. The nuances of fixed-income instruments are the subject of other books. The focus of this book is alternative investment strategies, so this chapter concentrates on the core strategy principles practiced by most fixed-income arbitrageurs.

CORE STRATEGY

FIXED-INCOME ARBITRAGEURS take offsetting long and short positions in similar fixed-income securities whose values are mathematically or historically interrelated, but in which that relationship is believed to be temporarily out of sync. These positions could include corporate debt, sovereign debt, municipal debt, or the sovereign debt of emerging market countries. Many times, trades will involve swaps and futures. When a bond or its derivative is sold short, the seller borrows that security and sells it immediately on the market with the intention of buying it back later at a lower price. By purchasing cheap fixed-income securities and selling short an equal amount of expensive fixed-income securities, fixed-income arbitrageurs attempt to protect themselves from changes in interest rates.

If they select instruments that respond to interest rate changes similarly, then an interest rate rise that adversely affects the long position will have an offsetting positive effect on the short position. They realize a profit when the skewed relationship between the securities returns to normal. Rather than try to guess in which direction the market will move, they neutralize interest rate changes and derive profit entirely from their ability to identify similar securities that are mispriced relative to one another.

Because the prices of fixed-income instruments are based on yield curves, volatility curves, expected cash flows, credit ratings, and special bond and option features, arbitrageurs must use sophisticated analytical models to identify true pricing disparities. They will assign probabilities to the different scenarios that they think can affect the pricing relationship, such as different interest rate environments or an international financial crisis, to narrow the universe of possible or likely outcomes. The complexity of fixed-income pricing is actually essential to fixed-income arbitrageurs. They rely on investors less sophisticated than themselves to over- and undervalue securities by failing to value explicitly some feature of the instrument (e.g., a call option) or the probability of a possible future occurrence (e.g., a political event) that will affect the valuation of the instrument.

One way fixed-income arbitrageurs compare different bond issues is by looking at their **YIELDS** and **YIELD CURVES**. A yield curve is a graphic representation of the yield to maturity at a given point in time for a variety of equally risky bonds differing in maturity. Because it is nearly risk free, the Treasury rate is used as a benchmark. Corporate bonds of a comparable maturity and comparable coupon rates will have higher yields than the treasuries to reflect greater default risk, so their yields are often quoted as a spread above the Treasury rate. The more risky the bond issue is, the larger the **SPREAD**. Spreads are measured in basis points. One basis point equals $\frac{1}{100}$ of a percent.

An example of a spread relationship is the Treasury-to-Eurodollar (TED) spread. U.S. Treasury notes, bills, and bonds are guaranteed and therefore are extremely low risk. Even though the European banks have very high credit ratings, and the U.S. government and the European banks are chasing the same dollars, the European banks have to pay a higher yield because their bonds are not guaranteed. Thus, when world financial markets are relatively stable and investors perceive the risk of European bank defaults to be extremely low, they will loan their dollars to European banks in exchange for the higher yield. As this happens, the TED spread will tighten. When conditions become unstable and investors do not perceive the spread to be large enough to compensate for the risks involved, then the same dollars will make their way back to safer U.S. Treasury instruments. If this state of affairs persists, then the TED spread will widen as the European banks offer more attractive yields to try to attract dollar deposits.

INVESTMENT PROCESS

FIXED-INCOME ARBITRAGEURS analyze fixed-income instruments' current yields and potential for capital appreciation to try to find valuation discrepancies. When they are able to determine a significant relationship between the yields of two or more bonds, establish that the relationship is out of sync, and determine that the probabilities that the relationship will return to normal or shift in a way that they anticipate are in their favor, they will simultaneously buy the undervalued security and sell short the overvalued security. After the positions are put on, the trade is monitored and then liquidated when the instruments reach their expected values. If they do not behave as expected, the positions will be reconsidered. Often, fixed-income arbitrageurs identify spread relationships that are only a few basis points from where they should be. To make a significant amount of money on the trade, arbitrageurs will apply a large amount of leverage to these positions. Because the downside risk on any one trade is small, the use of leverage does not increase risk dramatically.

MANAGER EXAMPLE

LET US REVISIT the TED spread. Suppose the price of a U.S. Treasury bill is 94.30 (implied yield of 5.70 percent) and the Eurodollar future is trading at 93.10 (implied yield of 6.90 percent). The TED spread is 94.30 - 93.10 = 1.20. The spread would be quoted as 120 (basis points). A fixed-income arbitrageur analyzes this spread and determines that it will widen further to 130 because of international financial worries. He or she would then buy T-bill futures and sell Eurodollar futures, expecting T-bill futures to outperform the market and Eurodollar futures to underperform it. This is known as *buying the spread*. Such a trade would unfold as follows:

Buy 10 T-bill futures contracts @ 94.30
Sell short 10 Eurodollar futures contracts @ 93.10
Spread = 120 basis points

As the fixed-income arbitrageur's analysis predicted, the spread widens to 130, with T bills now trading at 94.25 and Eurodollars at 92.95:

Sell 10 T-bill contracts @ 94.25
Buy 10 Eurodollar contracts @ 92.95
Spread = 130 points

Profit (from Eurodollars) = 15 basis points x $25 per basis point
    x 10 contracts = $3,750
Loss (from T-bills) = 5 basis points x $25 per basis point x 10
    contracts = $1,250
Net Profit = $2,500

MORTGAGE-BACKED SECURITIES

TO REITERATE A point made at the outset of this chapter, one of the newer additions to the universe of fixed-income securities is mortgage-backed securities (MBS). Like other fixed-income instruments, MBSs have certain properties of which fixed-income arbitrage strategies try to take advantage.

A mortgage-backed security represents an ownership interest in mortgage loans made by financial institutions such as savings and loans, commercial banks, or mortgage companies to finance the borrower's purchase of a home. Commercial banks, government agencies such as the Government National Mortgage Association (GNMA or Ginnie Mae), and government-sponsored enterprises such as the Federal National Mortgage Association (FNMA or Fannie Mae) will pool mortgage loans in a trust and issue securities that represent a direct ownership in that trust. Like traditional bonds, MBSs have an interest and a principal component. Unlike traditional bonds, MBSs have uncertain maturity dates because every mortgagee in the pool has the option to refinance or prepay the mortgage. Like traditional bonds, MBSs' prices fluctuate in response to interest rates. However, interest rates have an additional effect on them. Generally, when interest rates decline, prepayments accelerate beyond the initial pricing assumptions, which causes the average life and expected maturity of the MBS to shorten. However, when interest rates rise, prepayments slow down beyond the initial pricing assumptions and can cause the average life and expected maturity of the MBS to increase and its market value to decline. When prepayments increase because of a drop in interest rates, the principal of the security may have to be invested at a lower interest rate than the coupon of the security.

Although prepayments are a function of interest rates, they do not have a one-to-one relationship with new rates. Other prepayment factors, such as housing turnover, are much less influenced by interest rates than are refinancings. Thus, prepayment risk can be difficult to quantify. Because the borrower has the option to prepay the mortgage, MBSs contain an embedded option. The price that an investor must be paid to accept this option increases as the propensity to refinance increases. However, these securities are often mispriced because it is so difficult to predict prepayments exactly. Generally, MBSs have higher yields than traditional bonds because of prepayment risk.

Although MBSs may seem very different from traditional fixed-income instruments, fixed-income investors are looking for the same things in both. At the end of the day, investors must judge whether the reward that an instrument offers (coupon) at the price it is being offered (price of the security) is worth the risk associated with that instrument (whether it is credit risk, market risk, or prepayment risk). When the market over- or undervalues a security, an opportunity for arbitrage profits exists.

RISK CONTROL

AS DISCUSSED EARLIER, many fixed-income arbitrageurs try to insulate themselves from market risk by taking offsetting long and short positions in similar securities that are historically or statistically interrelated but for which the spread relationship is temporarily out of sync. Statistically interrelated refers to **DURATION.**

Duration is a measure of how sensitive a bond's price is to a shift in interest rates. For example, if a bond has a duration of three years, then the bond's value will decline 3 percent for each 1 percent increase in interest rates or rise 3 percent for each 1 percent fall in interest rates. Such a bond is less risky than a bond with a six-year duration, which will decline in value 6 percent for each 1 percent increase in interest rates and rise 6 percent for each 1 percent decrease. In general terms,

$$\text{Duration} = \frac{\text{(Change in price)/Price}}{\text{Change in interest rates}}$$

Duration is measured in years because it is equal to the average maturity of bonds for which that particular price/yield relationship holds. Bonds with longer maturities will be more affected by a change in interest rates because that change will be felt over a longer period of time. For example, if someone has a two-year bond with a coupon rate of 7 percent and a five-year bond with a similar rate of 7 percent and interest rates rise 1 percent, then both bonds are less attractive than they were at the time of purchase because the same interest rate is available now for less money. The price of the two-year bond reflects only the present value of its now less favorable rate over two years, whereas the five-year bond reflects the present value over five years. Accordingly, the price of a bond with a longer maturity will be more sensitive to changes in interest rates.

Fixed-income arbitrageurs often will buy a bond and sell short another bond with similar duration. That way, if interest rates change, the effect on the long position will be offset by the short position because both bonds respond the same way to the change. If the total duration of the long side of a portfolio is equal to the total duration of the short side of the portfolio, then the portfolio is said to have zero duration. Arbitrageurs will often try to eliminate market risk by structuring their trades and portfolios to be at or near zero duration. They can hedge out foreign currency risk in a similar fashion. In addition, they will usually minimize credit risk by only dealing in issues with high credit ratings. Finally, fixed-income arbitrageurs will usually maintain a diversified basket of trades so that the portfolio is not dependent on any one position. For the most part, they try to hedge away all the known risks. What is left is the risk that the mathematical relationship that they identify does not behave as they expected or was not out of sync in the first place.

MANAGER EXAMPLE

THIS TRADE EXAMPLE illustrates an on-the-run 30-year bond versus an old 30-year bond (forward basis). The objective of this trade is to capitalize on situations in which the spot market, in combination with the repo market, implies forward spreads that differ significantly from the current spot (i.e., the expected forward) market. The trading strategy is to sell the overvalued security in the forward market and buy the undervalued security on a leveraged basis. The risk is that conditions change dramatically between the current and future dates in an unexpected fashion (i.e., a fundamental change in the debt structure of the federal government).

The analysis of the historical spread relationship for similar bonds shows that in all the examined cases the spread ended up very close to one basis point. They expect that this relationship will hold in this case as well. The manager's strategy unfolded as follows:

Sell forward $500 million of $6\frac{1}{8}$ of 11/27 to 8/17/98
Buy forward $493 million of $6\frac{3}{8}$ of 8/27 to 8/17/98

4.1	POSSIBLE OUTCOMES OF TRADE		
FORWARD SPREAD	NEGATIVE CARRY	SPREAD PROFIT (LOSS)	TOTAL PROFIT (LOSS)
5.0	-$178,124	-$518,282	-$696,406
4.5	-$178,124	-$177,307	-$355,431
4.0	-$178,124	$163,668	-$14,465
3.5	-$178,124	$504,643	$326,519
3.0	-$178,124	$845,618	$667,494
2.5	-$178,124	$1,186,593	$1,008,469
2.0	-$178,124	$1,527,568	$1,349,444
1.5	-$178,124	$1,868,543	$1,690,419
1.0	-$178,124	$2,209,509	$2,031,394

Spot spread	4.5 (6.175 - 6.13)
Implied forward spread	4.24

Negative carry, 11/17/97 to 8/17/98	$178,124
Profit (loss) per 1-basis-point spread	$681,950

Figure 4.1 shows some of the possible outcomes of the trade. If the historical spread relationship holds, the result will produce one of the more positive results.[5]

ADVANTAGES/DISADVANTAGES

PRACTITIONERS OF fixed-income arbitrage can achieve consistently high returns without exposure to the ebb and flow of interest rates. The strategy has performed in a variety of economic conditions because it ferrets out trading anomalies rather than attempting to time interest rate changes. It is consistent and normally exhibits very low volatility. On the downside, identifying trading anomalies is no easy task considering the complexity of fixed-income instrument pricing. The need to sell securities short limits arbitrageurs to those markets where short selling is an option. Consequently, they tend to trade very liquid issues with high credit ratings that have very low default risk and can easily be sold short. These are the most efficient fixed-income markets; therefore the pricing relationships are less apt to be far out of sync. This means that these traders often must identify small discrepancies and apply heavy leverage to them.

The use of leverage also magnifies the risk of the position as well as creating additional risk. This was dramatically illustrated by Long Term Capital as well as by other highly leveraged hedge funds when theory met reality in 1998. Among other issues, highly leveraged bets on the relationship between government and corporate bonds went against expectations when the collapse of the Russian market helped trigger a market selloff and flight to quality from corporate into government bonds.

PERFORMANCE

FROM JANUARY 1990 to March 1998, fixed-income arbitrage funds registered average annualized returns of 12.32 percent, with an annualized standard deviation of 3.83. These returns are well above traditional fixed-income investments at a comparable level of risk. The high year was 1992 at 22.13 percent, and the low year was 1995 at 6.07 percent. In 1994, fixed-income arbitrage funds registered a 11.92 percent gain despite interest rate hikes that drove down bond prices. In the falling interest rate and rising stock market years that followed, the strategy actually did not fare as well. As evidenced by a correlation statistic of 0.0003, fixed-income arbitrage has very little sensitivity to stock market prices in general. The low correlation to market indices is expected because fixed-income arbitrageurs target pricing discrepancies rather than market movements *(see Appendix C for updated performance)*.

SUMMARY POINTS

PROFIT OPPORTUNITY

◆ Arbitrage is the practice of buying securities in one market and reselling similar securities simultaneously in another to profit

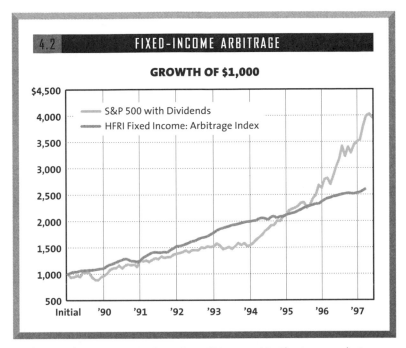

4.2 FIXED-INCOME ARBITRAGE

GROWTH OF $1,000

Legend:
— S&P 500 with Dividends
— HFRI Fixed Income: Arbitrage Index

x-axis: Initial, '90, '91, '92, '93, '94, '95, '96, '97
y-axis: $4,500, 4,000, 3,500, 3,000, 2,500, 2,000, 1,500, 1,000, 500

from a discrepancy in the price of the asset in the two markets.

◆ Because the prices of fixed-income instruments are based on yield curves, volatility curves, expected cash flows, credit ratings, and special bond and option features, the fixed-income arbitrageur must use sophisticated analytical models to identify true pricing disparities. The complexity of fixed-income pricing is what provides them with arbitrage opportunities.

◆ Practitioners of fixed-income arbitrage can achieve consistently high returns without exposure to the ebb and flow of interest rates. The strategy should work equally well in most economic conditions because it ferrets out trading anomalies rather than attempting to time interest rate changes. The high degree of leverage that is often used, however, can result in significant losses when abrupt market shifts collapse liquidity.

SOURCE OF RETURN

◆ Fixed-income arbitrageurs take offsetting long and short positions in similar fixed-income securities whose values are mathematically or historically interrelated, but in which that relationship is temporarily out of sync.

◆ Fixed-income arbitrageurs realize a profit when the skewed relationship between the securities behaves as they expect.

◆ Often fixed-income arbitrageurs identify spread relationships that are only a few basis points from where they should be. To make a significant amount of money on the trade, they will apply a large amount of leverage to these positions.

BUY/SELL PROCESS

◆ When fixed-income arbitrageurs are able to determine a significant relationship between the yield of two or more bonds, establish that the relationship is out of sync, and determine that the relationship will change in a way that they anticipate, they will simultaneously buy the undervalued security and sell short the overvalued security.

◆ Fixed-income arbitrageurs will buy a bond and sell short another bond with similar duration. That way, if interest rates change, then the effect on the long position will be offset by the short position, because both bonds respond the same way to the change.

◆ On the downside, identifying trading anomalies is no easy task considering the complexity of fixed-income instrument pricing. The need to sell securities short limits fixed-income arbitrageurs to those markets in which short selling is an option.

KEY TERMS

Arbitrage. The simultaneous purchase and sale of a security or pair of similar securities to profit from a pricing discrepancy.

Duration. A measure of how sensitive a bond's price is to a shift in interest rates. In general terms,

$$\text{Duration} = \frac{\text{(Change in price)/Price}}{\text{Change in interest rates}}$$

Fixed-income securities. Securities that entitle the holder to a series of fixed payments at predetermined future dates.

Mortgage-backed securities. Securities that represent an ownership interest in mortgage loans made by financial institutions (such as savings and loans, commercial banks, or mortgage companies) to finance the borrower's purchase of a home.

Prepayments. When mortgages are paid early, usually due to refinancing by the homeowner, investors receive principal payments ahead of the scheduled repayment date.

Spread. Corporate bonds of a comparable maturity and comparable coupon rates to treasuries will have higher yields to reflect greater default risk, so their yields are often quoted as a spread above the Treasury rate. The more risky the bond issue is, the larger the spread. Spreads are measured in basis points. One basis point equals $1/100$ of a percent.

Yield. The single investment rate that sets the present value of all a bond's future cash payments equal to the price of the bond.

CHAPTER

Equity Market
Neutral
(STATISTICAL ARBITRAGE)

EQUITY-MARKET-NEUTRAL statistical arbitrage strategists construct portfolios that consist of approximately equal dollar amounts of offsetting long and short equity positions. They use sophisticated quantitative and qualitative models to select stocks. Stocks expected to outperform the market are held long, and stocks expected to underperform the market are sold short. By balancing long and short positions, the market-neutral strategist insulates his or her portfolio from any systemic turn of events that affects valuations of the stock market as a whole. Such investors often apply the same logic across sectors, industries, and investment styles. Thus, market-neutral strategists derive profits from the ability of their models to pick over- and undervalued stocks, regardless of market direction.

EQUITY MARKET-NEUTRAL can be a deceptive name. Equity-market-neutral strategies are not without risk; they merely neutralize one kind of risk in favor of another. In equity portfolios, there are two primary sources of risk: stock selection and the market. Selecting stocks involves uncertainty about the fate of a particular stock. **MARKET RISK** is exposure to uncertainty about what the stock market as a whole will do next. Because they think they can predict the fate of a particular stock better than the direction of the market as a whole, equity-market-neutral specialists try to neutralize systemic risks associated with the market in favor of **STOCK SELECTION RISK**. They do so by taking a large number of long positions in stocks that they think will outperform the market and an offsetting amount of short positions in stocks that they think will underperform the market. Most practitioners of the strategy rely on quantitative, computer-run models. Equity-market-neutral specialists use these quantitative models to create a statistical advantage in picking stocks and a strategic advantage in controlling exposure to systemic risk. This approach is designed to produce consistent returns with very low volatility in a variety of market environments.

CORE STRATEGY

EQUITY-MARKET-NEUTRAL strategists will hold a large number of equity positions and an offsetting amount of short positions. They use sophisticated quantitative and qualitative models to pick stocks. Stocks expected to outperform the market are held long, and stocks expected to underperform the market are sold short. Equity-market-neutral strategists try to keep market exposure to a minimum. A simplified version of the formula that they use to calculate market exposure is shown below:

$$\text{Market exposure} = \frac{\text{Long exposure} - \text{Short exposure}}{\text{Capital}}$$

Equity-market-neutral strategists may extend this logic across sectors, industries, and investment styles. For example, if they take a long position in an information technology stock that they think is undervalued, then they will take an offsetting short position in an information technology stock that they think is overvalued. By being long and short in equal amounts, the equity-market-neutral strategist insulates the portfolio from any systemic turn of events that affects the information technology sector as a whole and emphasizes the ability of the chosen model to pick over- and undervalued stocks.

At the heart of most equity-market-neutral strategies is a proprietary multifactor model (econometric or otherwise) of equity risk and return that constructs an optimal portfolio while neutralizing systemic risks. Equity-market-neutral strategists capitalize on the power of these quantitative models to analyze financial data for large numbers of stocks over multiple factors. Because quantitative models can analyze such large amounts of data once they are constructed, equity-market-neutral strategists sometimes use the entire breadth of the market to protect themselves from its caprices. They take large numbers of positions because they believe that their statistical advantage in picking stocks is similar to the advantage that the house enjoys in blackjack: any one bet may go against it, but in the long run the odds are statistically in its favor.

INVESTMENT PROCESS

FIRST, EQUITY-MARKET-NEUTRAL specialists define a universe of stocks to be considered. This universe is usually made up of large, very liquid names because smaller, less liquid stocks are not always available to borrow and sell short, and equity-market-neutral portfolios experience high turnover. Furthermore, equity-market-neutral specialists consider a broad range of large-capitalization stocks because their quantitative models are not limited by the need to analyze each firm individually. Once their models are developed, they can look at any number of firms.

Next, an equity-market-neutral specialist applies a model to the defined universe of stocks. This model does two things: identifies the most relatively overvalued and relatively undervalued stocks in the universe, and defines the risk factors of owning those particular stocks. The model evaluates companies over a set of indicators or factors. The **INDICATORS** that are plugged into the model are usually based on publicly available information and conceptually sound and stable economic ideas about value, possess a good historical forecasting record, and have a low correlation with other indicators in the model. Indicators with more forecasting ability will be appropriately weighted in the model. According to Dr. John S. Brush, the chief investment officer of Columbine Capital Services, Inc., "The key is to determine which factors are consistently predictive, and what weightings those factors should receive in a multifactor model to best identify relative valuations."[6] A similar model is used to evaluate **SYSTEMIC RISK FACTORS**.

After evaluating the defined universe of stocks for both value and risk, the equity-market-neutral specialist creates the optimal bundle of equal amounts of undervalued and overvalued stocks while maintaining as close to a net zero exposure to the systemic risk factors as possible.

MANAGER EXAMPLE

"A CONSERVATIVE IMPLEMENTATION of equity-market-neutral investing can be seen by looking at some well-known stocks. The illustration offers examples of "paired" equity-market-neutral and "iterative" equity-market-neutral portfolio construction strategies.

General Motors (GM) and Ford offer a simple illustration of a "paired" equity-market-neutral strategy. From a risk perspective, they both make autos and have finance subsidiaries and international operations. If the investment selection process ranks Ford highly and General Motors poorly, the investor can go long Ford and short GM. It is easy to have equal dollar-weighted positions of these very liquid stocks. By replicating this long/short construction process in each of the other sectors, you have built a "paired" long/short strategy.

Paired strategies are understandable, but the opportunity for execution is limited. In reality, there are very few combinations of liquid stocks with opposite performance expectations and identical risk profiles in the same industry.

Consider the challenge presented by a favorable investment selection ranking of General Electric (GE). Holding this company as a long position could require many other firms to be sold short to maintain industry neutrality. GE is in a wide variety of businesses and does not fit into one industry. Their businesses include jet engine manufacturing, leasing, appliances, investment management, electrical distribution, industrial controls, plastics, broadcasting, and our friend the light bulb.

A manager who wants to be as close to neutral as quantifiably possible must offset a variety of market and industry risk factors. This calls for an "iterative" approach to portfolio construction. Rather than pairing a series of companies together into a portfolio, the long and short portfolios are viewed holistically. The key concern is that the risk characteristics of the long and short portfolios are mirror images. Quantitative risk characteristics can be used to create a risk sensitivity measure for each controlled factor. The long portfolio is built relative to the short portfolio, while the short portfolio is built relative to the long portfolio."[7]

MANAGER EXAMPLE

ONE OBVIOUS WAY to neutralize the portfolio is to "offset" stocks on an industry or sector basis. Go long the most attractive stock in the industry, and short the least attractive. This is a simple way to combine attractive return potential with risk minimization.

More comprehensively, this can be done at the portfolio level. The risk characteristics of the long and the short portfolio can be matched (beta risk, economic risk, interest rate risk, etc.) while building the optimal strategy.

An example from our history is fairly recent. For the past twelve to fifteen months, our models have favored large, high-quality, stable earnings producers. Much of that bias relates to the fact that we are in the late stages of a business cycle yet still enjoying stable interest rates in a low-inflation environment. At the same time we have concerns about foreign exchange rate risk, due to the rising dollar, the Asia crisis, and the volatility of the dollar. So from a return standpoint there is almost an inherent "conflict" in these views, since many of the large, high-quality, stable companies have significant international exposures. Hence, the portfolio manager has to decide on the importance of these attributes relative to each stock, balance the risk profile of each stock, and balance the transaction cost associated with each stock. Because of these complex interactions, computer algorithms are used to fully balance the portfolio.

The quantitative nature of equity-market-neutral strategies creates an image of a black box that, once established, runs of its own accord. In fact, equity-market-neutral specialists expend a great deal of time and resources to try to constantly improve and refine their models. At the trading level, they will rebalance their portfolios continuously to reflect the model's changing opinions of individual stocks and to maintain neutrality over the chosen risk factors. In addition, equity-market-neutral specialists must develop state-of-the-art trading systems that allow them to implement their model-driven strategies in a cost-effective manner. [8]

RISK CONTROL

EQUITY-MARKET-NEUTRAL specialists construct portfolios that consist of approximately equal dollar amounts of offsetting long and short positions to render the portfolio insensitive to market risk. The positions are based on a variety of risk production factors such as industry sectors, market capitalization, price to earnings, or beta. They emphasize small position size and widespread diversification to limit the damage any one position can have on the portfolio as a whole. They take positions in larger, more liquid companies to control short squeezes and liquidity risks. Most equity-market-neutral specialists actively manage risk in terms of stop-loss levels and target prices for individual positions to reduce the impact of any single position on the portfolio.

SHORT SELLING

EQUITY-MARKET-NEUTRAL specialists, by definition, actively engage in **SHORT SELLING**. As always, the major disadvantage of short selling is a limited upside and a theoretically infinite downside. When an investor borrows a stock and sells it short, he or she makes a profit when the price of the stock declines and loses money if it appreciates. Because the price of a stock can only decline to zero, the maximum profit on a short sale is the full

price of the stock at the time that it is sold short. However, the price of the stock can theoretically appreciate
an infinite amount.

In many markets, all stocks are not available to short.
Equity-market-neutral specialists try to get around this difficulty by screening the liquidity of stocks in their investment universe to eliminate stocks that are or will be in
short supply. Another worry for equity-market-neutral specialists is getting caught in a short squeeze. They try to
avoid short squeezes by taking short positions in stocks in
which investors have shown little interest. A positive feature of short selling is the interest that is collected after the
borrowed stock is sold and before buying it back, which is
called the short rebate. Nevertheless, short selling is a complicated trading process that requires resources to implement. Equity-market-neutral specialists try to build these
implementation costs into their models.

ADVANTAGES/DISADVANTAGES

EQUITY-MARKET-NEUTRAL strategies leverage manager
skills and the predictive power of quantitative models.
Because the approach is designed to pick both good and
bad stocks rather than time investment styles or industries, it is expected to work equally well in all economic
environments; however, performance will depend in part
on which factors have or have not been neutralized. It
offers the chance to make positive investment returns in a
down market, and theoretically eliminates the risk of substantive losses stemming from market decline. Equity-
market-neutral specialists argue that it would be virtually
impossible to construct a scenario where a large diversified portfolio of large, liquid U.S. stocks could decline
substantially in price without a similar significant price
decline taking place in the offsetting short positions within the same factor groups. In a worst-case scenario, the
value of every stock in the United States would go to zero
for a loss of 100 percent on the long positions and a similar gain of 100 percent for the short positions. The port-

folio would still achieve a positive return if the money from the short sales earned interest, discounting for margin interest.

Equity-market-neutral strategies generate returns on both the long and short sides; these returns have a low correlation to the returns of long-only market indices. Because of its low correlation to other asset classes, an equity-market-neutral strategy can provide diversification relative to those other asset classes.

PERFORMANCE

ON A RISK-ADJUSTED BASIS, equity-market-neutral funds performed very well in the 1990s. From January 1990 to March 1998, equity-market-neutral funds registered average annualized returns of 12.09 percent with an annualized standard deviation of 2.73. This low standard deviation is comparable with volatility measures for investment grade fixed-income instruments and is almost unheard of in an equity-only portfolio. Equity-market-neutral funds registered similarly low volatility on a month-to-month

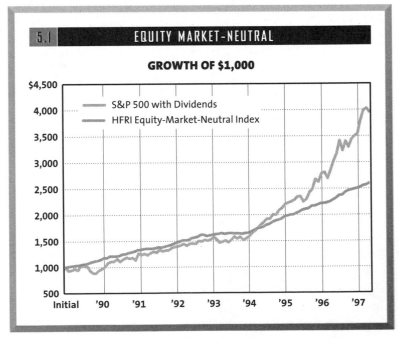

5.1 EQUITY MARKET-NEUTRAL

GROWTH OF $1,000

S&P 500 with Dividends
HFRI Equity-Market-Neutral Index

basis. They recorded a low of 2.65 percent return in 1994 and a solid 8.71 in 1992. The remainder of the years all had returns in the mid-teens *(see Appendix C for updated performance)*.

SUMMARY POINTS

PROFIT OPPORTUNITY

◆ Equity-market-neutral specialists use both long and short quantitative models to create a statistical advantage in picking stocks and a strategic advantage in controlling exposure to systemic risk by balancing the long and short exposure across a variety of market factors.

◆ They capitalize on the power of these quantitative models to analyze financial data for large numbers of stocks over multiple factors.

SOURCE OF RETURN

◆ Returns are generated from long positions in stocks that will outperform the market and short positions in stocks that underperform the market.

◆ Large numbers of positions are taken to benefit from the statistical advantages identified in the statistical models.

◆ Because the strategy is designed to pick both good and bad stocks rather than time investment styles or industries, it should work equally well in most economic environments. It offers the chance to make investment returns in a down market and theoretically eliminates the risk of substantive losses stemming from market decline.

INVESTMENT PROCESS

◆ A large number of long positions in stocks expected to outperform the market and an equal number of offsetting short positions in stocks expected to underperform the market are selected based on statistical models. These selections are then screened for elements that might be missed by the models before the positions are put on. Positions are reevaluated and rebalanced on a regular basis.

KEY TERMS

Equity-market-neutral portfolio. A portfolio composed of balanced exposure to long stock positions and offsetting short stock positions.

Indicators. Financial data used to forecast the future performance of a company.

Market exposure. The amount of a portfolio exposed to market risk because it is not matched by an offsetting position.

Short selling. The practice of borrowing a stock on collateral and immediately selling it on the market with the intention of buying it back later at a lower price.

Stock selection risk. Exposure to uncertainty about the future valuation of a particular stock.

Systemic or market risk. Exposure to uncertainty about systemic rises and falls in stock market prices that affect the prices of all stocks in a market or sector.

Systemic risk factors. Factors, such as interest rates or the price of oil, that have the ability to affect the valuation of a whole range of securities, or an entire market, if they change.

CHAPTER

Convertible
ARBITRAGE

ONVERTIBLE ARBITRAGE seeks to profit from the price relationship between convertible bonds and the underlying common stock. Convertible bonds are bonds that can be converted into a fixed number of shares of the issuing company's stock. They are hybrid securities with features of both bonds and stocks, and therefore their valuations reflect both types of instruments. Convertible arbitrageurs extract arbitrage profits from these complex pricing relationships by purchasing the convertible bond and selling short its underlying stock. Generally, the price of the convertible will decline less rapidly than the underlying stock in a falling equity market and will mirror the price of the stock more closely in a rising equity market.

CORE STRATEGY

INVESTMENT MANAGERS IDENTIFY mispriced convertible bonds that they judge to have a favorable total-return profile. A favorable total-return profile means that the convertible bond's price will decline less rapidly than the underlying stock in a falling equity market and will mirror the price of the stock more closely in a rising equity market *(see Table 6.1 below)*.

In this example, the total-return profile of the convertible bond is favorable because it captures most of the upward movement of the underlying equity but

6.1 TOTAL RETURN PROFILE			
CHANGE IN PRICE OF UNDERLYING EQUITY	UP 20%	UNCHANGED	DOWN 20%
Price of Underlying Equity	+20%	0%	-20%
Price of Convertible Bond	+16%	+5%	-4%

escapes a significant amount of the downside.

The example simplifies the pricing relationships of which convertible arbitrage specialists try to take advantage. To delve a bit deeper, it's important to examine the basic elements comprising the peculiar features of the convertible bond that make these arbitrage opportunities available.

CONVERTIBLE BOND BASICS

A CONVERTIBLE BOND is a corporate bond issued with a conversion feature that allows the holder to convert the bond into a fixed number of shares of the issuing company's underlying common stock at any time prior to maturity or redemption of the bond. Like a bond, a convertible bond has a coupon or guaranteed interest payment and a maturity date (on which the issuer will redeem the bond at par value). Some convertible bonds have a call feature which, after the call date, allows the issuer to redeem the bond at its discretion, but at specified prices, before the stated maturity date.

Because convertible bonds combine bond features with stock features, their valuation is also a hybrid of stock and bond valuations. The value of the bond component of a convertible is known as the investment value. The price of the convertible will not normally fall below its investment value because even if the stock component falls to zero, the convertible still has value as a bond due to its claim against company assets senior to stockholders. The stock conversion component of a convertible bond is called its latent warrant. The value of the convertible bond if it were to be converted to common stock is called its conversion value. Because the holder of a convertible bond can convert it into a predetermined number of shares of the issuer's common stock, the value of the convertible bond often strongly correlates with the value of the underlying equity. Thus, as the price of the common stock appreciates or depreciates, the convertible bond's valuation usually follows. The degree to which such a change in the value of the underlying equity is reflected in the value of the convertible bond depends on the convertible bond's premium over conversion value.

For example, if a bond trading at $1,000 (normal par value) can be converted into fifty shares of a $14 stock, then the conversion value would be $700 (50 x 14). The premium is the difference between the market or purchase price and the conversion value, or $300 (1,000 - 700). The conversion premium is usually expressed as a percentage of the conversion value. Thus, in this example the convertible bond had a 42.9 percent conversion premium (300/700). Generally, the higher a convertible bond's conversion premium, the less the price of the convertible bond will correlate with the price of the underlying common stock. Various factors affect a convertible bond's conversion premium—such as, convertibles with higher yields will have a higher conversion premium because the convertible acts more like a bond as it trades closer to the level at which the issuer could issue nonconvertible debt. Thus, in such cases, investors pay more for the yield component than the equity component, regardless of what price the common stock may trade for.

Because it is a hybrid security, a convertible bond will respond to different market forces than its underlying common stock. In fact, there is almost never a one-to-one correspondence between the price of a convertible bond and the price of its underlying common stock. For example, the price of a convertible bond will tend to move inversely to changes in interest rates because of its bond characteristics, whereas its underlying common stock will react to the perceived macroeconomic causes and effects of such interest rate fluctuations. There is no single formula for calculating the movement of an underlying security as a function of its corresponding convertible bond, only a range of factors that have varying levels of predictive value. Convertible bond specialists make arbitrage profits by identifying pricing disparities between convertible bonds and their underlying equity and tightly monitoring the factors that will change these relationships.

INVESTMENT PROCESS

CONVERTIBLE BOND SPECIALISTS screen hundreds of convertible bonds to identify ones that are undervalued or mispriced relative to their underlying common stock. They may look at company fundamentals to identify future potential and the credit aspects of the bond. Some of the factors they consider may be premium-to-conversion ratio, call provisions on the bond, creditworthiness of the issuer (probability of default), yield advantage, and the company's earnings momentum. When they identify an undervalued or mispriced convertible bond, they will purchase the convertible and sell short the underlying common stock, creating a neutral position that can make money in a number of market conditions.

When a stock is sold short, the seller borrows that stock and immediately sells it on the market with the intention of buying it back later at a lower price. The cash proceeds from the sale are held in a money market account earning interest. This interest is known as a short interest rebate. If the stock pays a dividend, the convertible arbitrage specialist must pay the dividend. If the price of the stock falls, the convertible arbitrage specialist makes profits equal to the amount of the price decline multiplied by the number of shares sold short. Conversely, if the price of the stock rises, the convertible arbitrage specialist will realize losses equal to the amount the stock appreciates multiplied by the number of shares sold short.

When convertible arbitrage specialists sell short the underlying equity of a convertible bond, they hedge against a decline in the price of the stock. The amount of stock sold short is nearly always less than the full conversion amount, because this allows the position to retain profit potential on the upside. The number of shares sold short depends on how much market exposure they want. In a bear market approach, these specialists will sell a large percentage of the conversion amount short, forgoing any upside potential so that they can make profits in a falling equity market. In a bull market approach, they will sell less than is required for risk neutrality, allowing them to make more profits from equity appreciation. The number of shares they decide to sell short out of the total number possible is called the **HEDGE RATIO**. A hedge ratio that does not add exposure to up or down markets is called a *neutral hedge*. To determine the hedge ratio that will achieve the risk/reward characteristics they seek to attain, convertible arbitrage specialists look at stock prices, yield curve shifts, dividend yield, and volatility of the stock.

MANAGER EXAMPLE

A CONVERTIBLE ARBITRAGE specialist purchases ten convertible bonds at 120 ($120 per $100 par, so $1,200 x 10 = $12,000). The bond's coupon is 6 percent (each bond pays $60 per year, for a total of $600 for the ten bonds). The conversion ratio is 90 (each bond can be converted into ninety shares of common stock). The current price of the common stock is $12. The interest rate for funds held in a money market account (the short rebate interest rate) is 3 percent. The common stock does not pay dividends.

In this example, the convertible arbitrage specialist maintains an approximately neutral hedge ratio of 75 percent. Table 6.2 on the following page shows how price changes affect the overall return to a convertible arbitrage position.

In column A, although the stock price declines by 50 percent to $6, the convertible bond price declines by only 33 percent to $80, because the valuation favors the bond component as the stock component decreases in value. The decline in the price of the bond results in a loss of $4,000. However, the short sale of stock more than offset this loss by generating a profit of $4,500. Therefore, the net trading profit in this scenario is $500. In all the scenarios, the static return remains constant at $870. The total return on the position in scenario A is $1,370 or 11.4 percent (1,370/12,000).

In scenario B, neither the price of the stock nor the price of the convertible bond changes. Therefore, the

6.2   CONVERTIBLE ARBITRAGE EXAMPLE

THE STRATEGIES

Bonds Purchased	10 @ 120 = $12,000
Coupon	6% ($60 x 10) = $600
Conversion Ratio	90 shares per bond @ $12
Hedge Ratio	75% (750 shares @ $12/per share) = $9,000
Short Rebate	3% of 9,000 = $270

THE SCENARIOS

	PURCHASE PRICE	PRICE CHANGE OVER TWELVE MONTHS			
		A	B	C	D
Stock	$12	$6	$12	$18	$13
Convertible Bond	$120	$80	$120	$170	$116
Bond Coupon	$600	$600	$600	$600	$600
Short Rebate	$270	$270	$270	$270	$270
Static Profit/Loss	$870	$870	$870	$870	$870
Bond Profit/Loss		$(4,000)	0	$5,000	$(400)
Stock Profit/Loss		$4,500	0	$(4,500)	$(750)
Trading Profit/Loss		$500	0	$500	$(1,150)
TOTAL PROFIT/LOSS		$1,370	$870	$1,370	$(280)
as a Percentage of Capital		11.4%	7.2%	11.4%	-2.3%

profit comes solely from the static returns of $870 or 7.2 percent (870/12,000).

In scenario C, the stock price increases by 50 percent to $18. Because convertible bonds have a tendency to move more in line with the prices of their underlying stocks as the stock price increases, the price of the convertible bond increases by 42 percent to $170. The increase in the price of the bond results in a profit of $5,000. In addition, the loss on the short sale of stock is only $4,500 because only 75 percent of the warrant was sold short. The net trading profit in this scenario is $500. The total return on the position in scenario C is $1,370 or

11.4 percent (1,370/12,000)—the same as in scenario A.

In scenario D, the stock and convertible bond prices do not move in relation to one another as the convertible arbitrage specialist expected. The price of the convertible bond drops by 3 percent to $116 due to factors other than a decline in the value of the underlying stock, while the price of the stock increases to $13. This event-risk produces a trading loss on both the convertible bond and the short sale of the underlying stock that totaled $1,150. The net loss after the static return is $280 or 2.3 percent (280/12,000).[9]

RISK CONTROL

CONVERTIBLE ARBITRAGE SPECIALISTS try to invest in convertible bonds whose prices will decline less rapidly than the underlying stock in a falling equity market and will mirror the price of the stock more closely in a rising equity market. When they can identify such securities, they can make nice investment returns with little to no risk. However, this is not always possible because the pricing relationship does not always hold.

Two factors may disrupt the pricing relationship: the market or an issue specific to the company. At the market level, shifts in stock market volatility, interest rate changes, foreign exchange relationships, and political events can affect the relationship that the convertible arbitrage specialist expected would hold between the convertible bond and its underlying stock. Market risk is controlled by constructing portfolios that will stand up to a variety of different scenarios. At the company level, improving or weakening credit quality, short stock buy-ins, call features, dividend increases that reduce the cash flow component of the convertible bond, and corporate events such as takeovers and recapitalizations can alter the relationship between the convertible bond and its underlying stock. Issue-specific risks are controlled by diversifying the portfolio, doing in-depth credit analyses of each company, and actively hedging positions.

ADVANTAGES/DISADVANTAGES

CONVERTIBLE ARBITRAGE ALLOWS an investment manager to benefit from a bond yield and stock and bond price movements, regardless of market direction. It provides a static return from its coupon and the short interest rebate, regardless of stock and bond price movements. These returns can be augmented by trading returns if the convertible arbitrage specialist can identify undervalued or mispriced securities and successfully predict the future relationship between the price of these convertible bonds and their underlying stock. Hedging with common stock allows the convertible arbitrage specialist to design a strategy that has the ability to meet a wide range of investment objectives. Depending on what kind of hedge is preferred (bearish, neutral, bullish), the investment manager can create anything from a high-performance alternative to money markets to a conservative alternative to owning common stock to a low-risk alternative to short selling.

If the expected price relationships do not hold, the convertible arbitrage specialist can lose both on the bond and on the stock component of a convertible bond. This is a very real possibility because there is almost never a one-to-one correspondence between the price of a convertible bond and the price of its underlying common stock. In addition, for small-cap stocks, not all stocks are available to short so the universe of convertibles securities to choose from is somewhat limited.

PERFORMANCE

CONVERTIBLE ARBITRAGE FUNDS produced very steady, low-risk returns in the 1990s. From January 1990 to March 1998, they registered average annualized returns of 11.86 percent with an annualized standard deviation of 3.24. These returns are well above traditional fixed income investments at a comparable level of risk. In 1994, convertible arbitrage funds registered a 3.74 percent loss because interest rate hikes negatively affected the bond attributes of convertible bonds and also put pressure on the conversion premiums in anticipation of a drop in stock prices. Had stock prices dropped as expected, convertible arbitrage funds would have made profits on the short sale of stock that would have offset the negative impact of the interest rate increases. However, the equity sell-off never came, so the strategy suffered an off year. In the falling interest rate and rising stock market years that followed, the strategy produced steady returns in the mid-teens. As evidenced by a correlation statistic of 0.1287, convertible arbitrage has very little sensitivity to stock market prices in general *(see Appendix C for updated performance)*.

SUMMARY POINTS

PROFIT OPPORTUNITY

◆ Convertible bonds are hybrid securities that have features of a bond and of stock, and therefore their valuations reflect both types of instruments.

◆ Arbitrage opportunities arise when pricing discrepancies exist between the bond and the underlying equity. Such opportunities can be exploited by buying the convertibles and selling short the underlying common stock.

SOURCE OF RETURN

◆ Convertible bond specialists make arbitrage profits by identifying pricing disparities between convertible bonds and their underlying equity and tightly monitoring the factors that will change these relationships.

INVESTMENT PROCESS

◆ When convertible bond specialists identify an undervalued or mispriced convertible bond, they will purchase the convertible and sell short the underlying common stock, creating a neutral position that can make money in a number of market conditions.

◆ When a convertible arbitrage specialist sells short the underlying equity of a convertible bond, he or she hedges against a decline in the price of the stock.

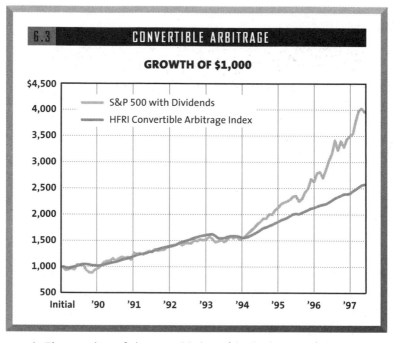

6.3 **CONVERTIBLE ARBITRAGE**

GROWTH OF $1,000

◆ The number of shares sold short (the hedge ratio) depends on how much exposure the convertible arbitrage specialist wants to the market.

KEY TERMS

Convertible arbitrage. The simultaneous purchase of a convertible bond and sale of the common stock to profit from a pricing discrepancy.

Call feature. A feature that allows the issuer to redeem the bond before it matures.

Conversion value. The value of the convertible bond if it were to be converted to common stock.

Convertible bond. A corporate bond issued with a conversion feature that allows the holder to convert the bond into a fixed number of shares of the issuing company's common stock.

Coupon. A bond's fixed interest payment.

Hedge ratio. The number of shares that the convertible arbitrage specialist decides to sell short out of the total number possible.

Investment value. The value of the bond component of a convertible bond.

Maturity date. The date on which a bond is redeemed (a five-year bond comes to maturity five years after it is issued).

Par value. The face value of a bond, or the amount for which it is redeemed at maturity.

Short interest rebate. The interest earned on the cash proceeds of a short sale of stock.

Static return. The interest income from coupon payments and short interest rebates that is unaffected by price fluctuations of convertible bonds and their underlying stock.

Warrant. The stock conversion component of a convertible bond.

CHAPTER

Merger (Risk)
ARBITRAGE

ISK OR MERGER *arbitrage specialists invest in companies that are being acquired or are involved in a merger. Typically, they will buy the common stock of a company being acquired or merging with another company and sell short the stock of the acquiring company. The target company's stock will usually trade at a discount to the value that it will attain after the merger is completed because all mergers take time and involve some risk that the transaction will not occur. If the transaction fails, then the price of the target company's stock usually declines. Merger arbitrage specialists make profits when they correctly anticipate the outcome of an announced merger and capture the spread between the current market price of the target company's stock and the price to which it will appreciate if the deal is completed.*

WHEN A MERGER is pending, uncertainty about the outcome creates a pricing disparity between the price of the acquiring company's stock and the price of the target company's stock. If the announced deal is completed, the two stocks will eventually represent ownership interests in the same company. Until the deal is consummated, there is typically a spread between the prices of the two stocks that reflects both the market's uncertainty about whether the deal will occur and the time value of money.

Because their outcomes are uncertain, mergers and acquisitions provide a particular kind of arbitrage opportunity. Traditional investment funds can only profit from these opportunities in a cursory way because they are restricted from short selling. However, merger arbitrage specialists use hedging strategies and specialized knowledge of merger and acquisition processes to extract arbitrage profits from the pricing discrepancies that result when potential mergers or acquisitions are announced.

CORE STRATEGY

IN STOCK SWAP MERGERS, risk or merger arbitrage specialists buy the common stock of a company being acquired or merging with another company and hedge the position by selling short the stock of the acquiring company. In a cash transaction, hedging may be done indirectly or not at all. During negotiations the target company's stock will typically trade at a discount to its value after the merger is completed because all mergers involve some risk that the transaction will not occur. If the transaction fails, then the price of the target company's stock usually declines. Profits are made by capturing the spread between the current market price of the target company's stock and the price to which it will appreciate when the deal is completed.

Merger arbitrage specialists do not try to anticipate possible mergers. Instead, they research announced mergers and acquisitions to reduce uncertainty about possible outcomes. They will try to ascertain the probability of new bidders for the target company after the announcement. Before taking a position, merger arbitrage specialists will consider public corporate documents, analyst reports, standard media releases, and conversations with companies and industry contacts. If the reward outweighs the risk of the deal failing, then they may invest in the situation. Generally, they will add to positions as more information becomes available and the outcome of the transaction becomes more certain. They will liquidate an investment position either when the rewards do not offset the perceived risks or when the transaction is consummated.

INVESTMENT PROCESS

THE SIMPLEST EXAMPLE of a merger arbitrage opportunity is a company being acquired for cash. The target company's stock will typically trade at slightly less than the price proposed by the acquiring company, reflecting the market uncertainty of the transaction being completed. An investor who purchases the target company's stock will receive this discount when the deal is completed.

In what are known as **STOCK-FOR-STOCK MERGERS**, the holders of the target company's stock receive shares of the acquiring company's stock rather than cash. In a normal stock-for-stock merger situation, a merger arbitrage specialist will sell the acquiring company's stock short and purchase a long position in the target company in the ratio of the proposed transaction to lock in the spread (if the purchasing firm is offering one-half share of its stock for every share of the target company, then the specialist will sell half as many shares of the purchasing firm as he or she buys of the target company).

Merger transactions are often complex, such as when the exchange ratio is based on the price of the acquiring company's stock when the deal is closed, but they generally combine elements of cash purchases and stock swaps. Typically, the outcome of more complex mergers is less certain, and therefore the spread is larger in these cases. Hostile takeovers and multiple bidder situations also make for larger spreads.

MANAGER EXAMPLE

ON FEBRUARY 26, 1997, 3Com (COMS), a computer networking company, announced the acquisition of US Robotics (USRX), a manufacturer of computer networking equipment and handheld devices. Each USRX share would be converted to 1.75 shares of COMS, a 12 percent premium to the market. The day of the announcement, 3Com sold off dramatically, falling 4 points (more than 10 percent) over concerns about dilution and strategic fit. As a result of the fall in COMS, the premium was completely erased and USRX closed down one-half point on the day of the announcement.[10]

THE STRATEGY

Long Position: 10,000 shares of USRX at $59.125
Short Position: 17,500 shares of COMS at $35
Hedge Ratio: 1.75
Close of Transaction: 6/13/97
USRX: $83.23[11]   Profit: $241,050
COMS: $47.56   Loss: $219,800
Profit: $21,250
Rate of Return: $21,250 / (10,000 x $591,250)   = 3.59%
Annualized Rate of Return: = 12.25%

ADVANTAGES/DISADVANTAGES

MERGER ARBITRAGE IS mainly event driven rather than market driven. Merger arbitrage returns, therefore, are not strongly correlated to overall stock market movement. A group of merger arbitrage specialists can achieve high returns over time based on the ability to anticipate the probable outcome of specific transactions as opposed to the far more random nature of most directional investment strategies.

Although they are not correlated to overall stock market movements, merger arbitrage returns still depend on the overall volume of merger activity, which has historically been cyclical in nature. Because merger activity can be cyclical, merger arbitrage specialists may have a hard time diversifying their portfolios during down periods. Often, merger arbitrage is used as one component of a more general event-driven strategy.

INDUSTRY CHANGES

ALTHOUGH THE OVERALL volume of mergers exploded in the 1990s, fewer and fewer of them are leveraged buyouts and hostile takeovers. Because of the prevailing bull market, firms have had more capital than ever before with which to make deals. Today, most mergers are strategic and noncompetitive. In strategic transactions, the acquirer has a good business reason for the merger and has a strong sense of how much value the target company will add. The number of such transactions grew because many companies increased their efficiency in the early 1990s and as a result were enjoying high profitability, strong cash flow, and anticipated expansion. These companies plan on acquiring other companies because they find it cheaper to buy market share than to build it. Companies are also consolidating to stay globally competitive and in response to rapid regulatory changes. A good example is the banking industry, which is consolidating as the barriers to interstate commerce collapse. Another factor affecting the overall volume and kind of mergers is the manner in which a company's management is compensated. Managers' interests are more closely aligned than ever with those of shareholders because of the high percentage of their total compensation represented by stock options. Because stock options create real potential for managers to increase their personal wealth, many have become more willing to consider business alternatives that will create shareholder value, including selling or merging the firm.

All this is mixed news for merger arbitrage specialists. Although there are more opportunities, strategic non-competitive mergers lead to smaller investment spreads. In financial or hostile takeover situations, the buyers sometimes are less disciplined and more inclined to overpay for an acquisition. Obviously, multiple bidder situations are ideal because the ultimate takeover value will be driven substantially above the initial bid.

PERFORMANCE

FROM JANUARY 1990 to March 1998, merger (risk) arbitrage averaged an annualized rate of return of 13.21 percent, with an annual standard deviation of 4.32. This is a lower rate of return than the Standard and Poor's (S&P) 500 index of blue-chip stocks, which averaged more than 18 percent for the same period but with substantially lower risk. The S&P 500 index had an annualized standard deviation of more than 12, whereas the HFRI merger arbitrage

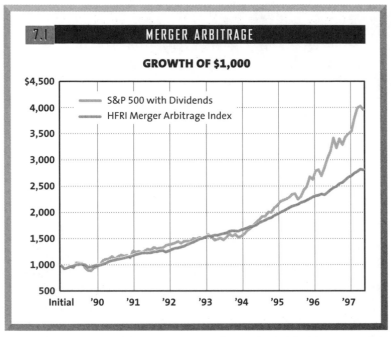

7.1   MERGER ARBITRAGE

GROWTH OF $1,000

Legend:
- S&P 500 with Dividends
- HFRI Merger Arbitrage Index

(Y-axis: $4,500 / 4,000 / 3,500 / 3,000 / 2,500 / 2,000 / 1,500 / 1,000 / 500)

(X-axis: Initial, '90, '91, '92, '93, '94, '95, '96, '97)

index deviated from its mean by only 4.30. Merger arbitrage produced a 0.44 percent return in the recession of 1990 and returns of 7.89 and 8.88 percent in 1992 and 1994. Otherwise, it produced a solid 16 to 20 percent throughout the 1990s. In addition, the HFRI merger arbitrage index registered a correlation statistic of 0.1553, which means that the index had a low sensitivity to changes in the prices of the stock market as a whole *(see Appendix C for updated performance)*.

SUMMARY POINTS

PROFIT OPPORTUNITY

◆ Financial traders profit from discrepancies in the market's pricing of an asset or two interrelated assets.

◆ Merger arbitrage specialists use specialized knowledge of merger and acquisition processes and hedging strategies to extract arbitrage profits from the pricing discrepancies that result when potential mergers or acquisitions are announced.

SOURCE OF RETURN

◆ Merger arbitrage specialists profit by capturing the spread between the current market price of the target company's stock and the price to which it will appreciate if the deal is completed.

◆ If the spread is favorable, merger arbitrage specialists buy the common stock of a company being acquired or merging with another company and, when appropriate, sell short the stock of the acquiring company.

◆ Merger arbitrage profits are dependent on the overall volume of these types of transactions rather than market direction (event driven rather than market driven).

INVESTMENT PROCESS

◆ Merger arbitrage specialists analyze the possible outcomes of announced deals rather than attempt to anticipate or identify companies to be involved in future mergers.

◆ In a normal stock swap merger situation, a merger arbitrage specialist sells the acquiring company's stock short and purchases a long position in the target company in the ratio of the proposed transaction to lock in the spread.

◆ Typically, the outcomes of more complex mergers are less certain, and therefore the spread will be larger.

KEY TERMS

Cash merger. A deal in which the acquiring company pays cash for the target company.

Leveraged buy-out. An often hostile situation in which the acquiring company buys out the target company by using borrowed funds.

Spread. The difference between the current market price of the target company's stock and the price to which it will appreciate if the deal is completed.

Stock-for-stock or stock swap merger. A deal in which the holders of the target company's stock receive shares of the acquiring company's stock rather than cash.

Strategic acquisition. A generally noncompetitive situation in which the acquiring company has a good business reason for the merger, such as expanding production capability or growing market share.

CHAPTER

Distressed
SECURITIES

ISTRESSED SECU-
rities specialists invest in the securities of companies
that are experiencing financial or operational
difficulties. Distressed situations include reorganizations, bankruptcies, distressed sales, and other
corporate restructurings. The pricing of these
securities is often distorted because many traditional
buyers either legally or customarily must sell the
securities of troubled companies. Therefore, a pricing
discount occurs that reflects both these structural
anomalies and uncertainty about the outcome of the
event. Depending on the manager's style, he or she
may invest in bank debt, corporate debt, trade claims,
common stock, or warrants.

The securities of a company suffering from financial
difficulties often trade below their intrinsic value
because of uncertainty about the future of the
company. Moreover, traditional investment funds are

often limited in their ability to hold these potentially undervalued securities by policy restrictions and regulatory constraints that do not now allow them to own securities with very low credit ratings. Hedge fund managers who specialize in distressed securities combine specialized knowledge of the bankruptcy process and fundamental analysis of companies and industries to extract investment returns from the pricing distortions placed on sound companies with bad capital structures. Their investment mandate and willingness to tolerate long periods of illiquidity allows them to cope with the vagaries of distressed securities.

CORE STRATEGY

DISTRESSED SECURITIES SPECIALISTS find investment opportunities in companies undergoing financial or operational difficulties. Usually, the distressed company is in some stage of negotiating a financial corporate reorganization or has filed for bankruptcy. These financial problems can occur from three major sources: operational problems, significant legal liability, or major management upheaval. If it has a strong core business, the company's management and creditors will try to deleverage the balance sheet. As a consequence of the reorganization, investors generally exchange their existing debt for a combination of equity and debt, with the new debt carrying a lower interest rate than the original debt. Distressed securities specialists will buy the securities if they believe that the company will return to historical profit levels after the reorganization because management will be free to focus on operations and reduce uncertainty about the future of the company. Although the turnaround time can be several years, they believe that a combination of new management, appropriate capital reinvestment, and a less onerous debt structure will encourage an upward evaluation of the company. The recovery process generally involves several major steps. Each one of these steps can provide an investment opportunity when an **EXIT CATALYST**, an event that may change the market's perception of (and therefore the value of) the distressed company, leads to higher valuations of the company's securities. An exit catalyst, in this context, usually involves the company passing a significant milestone on its path to recovery.

CORPORATE FINANCE AND BANKRUPTCY BASICS

TO GROW, COMPANIES need capital. They raise capital through either debt or equity financing. To the extent that a company is engaged in a speculative or risky business venture, it will have to pay a higher yield to attract bond purchasers. A company is said to be **HIGHLY LEVERAGED** if its ratio of debt payments to cash flow is high. When a company can no longer pay the principal or interest due to its bondholders (a process known as **SERVICING DEBT**), it is said to be in default. Companies with otherwise successful business operations go into default primarily for two reasons: bad capital structure and adverse outside events. In the first case, the company simply takes on more debt than it can service. In the second case, the company is pushed into default by an outside event such as a large cash award against it in a liability lawsuit. In either case, the company must make an arrangement with its creditors.

If the company reorganizes, it usually operates under Chapter XI of the U.S. Bankruptcy Code. If the company liquidates, it operates under Chapter VII of the U.S. Bankruptcy Code. In a liquidation scenario, the proceeds from the sale are allocated to the holders of the company's securities, with preferential payments made in order of seniority. The total proceeds generated by a **LIQUIDATION** are significantly less than the value of the enterprise if the company can continue to operate. Therefore, creditors often have a financial incentive to allow a company that has defaulted to reorganize. The company can work out an arrangement with its creditors outside the bankruptcy or within it. Within bankruptcy, the bankruptcy code (Chapter XI) protects a company from its creditors, which allows the company to reorganize its capital structure in a way that enables it to become profitable again. The new capital structure can take many forms, but usually debt is converted into equity.

INVESTMENT PROCESS

DISTRESSED SITUATIONS PROVIDE the opportunity to buy securities at a greatly discounted price because of **STRUCTURAL ANOMALIES**. Many institutions will not hold a company's bonds when that company is in financial difficulty. As the credit quality of a distressed company deteriorates, the price of its securities often reflects selling pressures created by investment policy restrictions, regulatory constraints, and window dressing for year-end investment holdings. Such artificial selling pressure distorts the bonds' prices.

Distressed securities specialists make investment returns on two kinds of mispricings: **FUNDAMENTAL** or **INTRINSIC**

VALUE, which is the actual value of the company that the bond interest represents and **RELATIVE VALUE**, which is the value of the bonds relative to the value of other securities of the same company. When the market price of a company's security is lower than its fundamental value because the company is experiencing temporary financial difficulties, distressed securities specialists will take core positions in these securities and hold them through the restructuring process, because they believe that the security will approach its "real" value after the restructuring is complete. While a company is restructuring, the prices of its different financial instruments can become mispriced relative to one another. This is an opportunity for what distressed securities specialists call *intracapitalization* or *capital structure arbitrage*. They will purchase the undervalued security and take short trading positions in the overpriced security to extract arbitrage profits.

Distressed securities specialists are better equipped than other investors to take advantage of these opportunities, because they can combine financial analysis of the fundamental value of distressed companies with specialized knowledge of the bankruptcy process that allows them to predict, and when necessary take steps to influence, the outcome of bankruptcies and reorganizations. They use information drawn from Wall Street research, marketplace contacts, publications, databases, financial and legal due diligence, and their own valuation models to estimate the fundamental value of distressed companies.

The greatest advantage that distressed securities specialists have over other investors in distressed situations is their specialized knowledge of the bankruptcy and out-of-court restructuring processes. When a company restructures in a typical Chapter XI situation, some of its debt is converted into equity. Therefore, the various involved parties must negotiate how to value that equity. Moreover, the bankruptcy code requires that the most senior creditors be repaid in full before any payment is provided to junior creditors. Consequently, the senior creditors' normal negotiating strategy is to **1** seek cash, **2** obtain the majority of their claim in new securities, or **3** demand new equity ownership based on current performance. They often succeed because the company is being valued at the bottom of the business cycle. Distressed security specialists have intimate knowledge of these kinds of negotiating and restructuring processes and can assess whether the company's problems can be resolved outside bankruptcy and how the company must restructure its capital. They also know the major players in the processes: bankruptcy lawyers, accountants, turnaround managers, and distressed securities investors. Their industry expertise allows them to forecast the outcome of specific restructurings and judge whether a given company's securities are overvalued or undervalued.

PHASES OF THE BANKRUPTCY PROCESS

DISTRESSED SPECIALISTS CHOOSE to invest at different phases of the bankruptcy cycle depending on their risk/reward tolerance. Much of this decision is dictated by how willing they are to become involved in the bankruptcy process. The early stages of bankruptcy tend to be chaotic. Traditionally, the courts have extended the almost exclusive control of the process to the company's existing management for at least six months to one year. During that time, the company's cash flow rises because management controls receipts and can postpone payments to creditors. However, during this initial period the management must propose plans for reorganization. The holders of the company's securities critically review these plans. Thus, the early stages of bankruptcy are contentious and unpredictable.

On a selective basis, distressed securities specialists often play an active role in restructuring distressed companies. In such cases, they may join the company's creditors committee or the board of directors. Before getting involved, they determine what the likely exit catalyst in the restructuring process will be. If they can add value by creating or facilitating an exit catalyst, then they will play an active role if the value that is added outweighs the opportunity cost of getting involved. Restructurings are very time intensive, so the manager who is involved will need to allocate time away from other aspects of business, such as finding new investments. Also, the manager cannot trade the company's securities while on the committee due to the privileged nature of the information provided to committee members. The distressed securities specialist weighs these disadvantages against the sometimes overwhelming advantages of being able to control and influence a situation to maximize potential returns. Manager involvement indicates a long term commitment; it is essential that the manager have a large pool of committed capital so that liquidity is not a problem.

LEVEL OF THE CAPITAL STRUCTURE

A DISTRESSED COMPANY'S securities fall along a risk spectrum that runs from the least risky (bank debt and senior corporate debt) to the most risky (common stock). Positions are sometimes hedged by taking a position long senior debt securities and at the same time short the equity of the same company. The core strategy is to buy the securities that provide the most attractive risk/reward ratio. Sometimes, distressed specialists will roll down a company's capital structure from senior debt to preferred or common equity as the company's financial situation improves and clarifies.

RISK CONTROL

DISTRESSED SECURITIES SPECIALISTS control risk through portfolio diversification, hedging techniques, and little, if any, use of leverage. In fact, brokers generally will not lend against bankrupt security holdings. Portfolios are diversified across assets and industries and over business cycles. Most managers cap the amount of their portfolio that can be held in any one position. They monitor risk by defining specific events that they anticipate and a valuation target and revisiting the investment if events do not transpire as anticipated or the target valuation is reached. Market risk may be hedged with index options, but it is generally a long strategy. Event risk can be hedged by having long and short holdings, but often the price volatility of an instrument is accepted as a risk that should not be managed. For clients that require certain levels of liquidity, the specialist will also monitor the overall liquidity of the portfolio.

MANAGER EXAMPLE

IN THE EARLY 1990s, Queens Moat Houses was one of the United Kingdom's and Europe's largest hotel chains. The company had embarked on a series of haphazard and expensive acquisitions in the mid- to-late 1980s. The European economic downturn of the early 1990s caused a significant decline in the company's cash flows and asset values. On October 29, 1993, Queens Moat Houses reported a loss in excess of 1 billion pounds sterling.

The company emerged from a long, contentious financial restructuring in June 1995. Many of its noncore properties and businesses had been sold off and the company reorganized around its U.K., German, Dutch, and French hotel units. The new balance sheet was substantially deleveraged, and several of the new debt securities, including the junior term debt, would not pay current interest for a number of years. As a result, even after operations began to improve in 1996 and early 1997, the junior term debt continued to trade at a substantial discount to the face value because it was not slated to pay interest until June 1999.

Trading at 61 cents on the dollar in early 1997, the junior term debt represented the most attractive security in the capital structure according to the company's analysis. First and foremost, it offered significant downside protection. They believed that the private market value of the U.K. operations alone, which approximated 70 percent of the company's operating cash flow in 1996, would cover the junior term debt up to 50 cents on the dollar. Second, the sale of several poorly performing properties in Germany confirmed the valuation of the company's hotels outside the United Kingdom, which were just beginning to emerge from economic hard times on the continent. Finally, the improvement in the cash flow of the continental European hotel assets reinforced the company management's view that the junior term debt was well covered by the asset value of the company.

As a result of their analysis, the company purchased junior term debt at 61 cents on the dollar in early 1997. As continental European operations continued to improve, investors gained more confidence in the ability of the company to pay its coupon on the junior term debt in June 1999, and the security has recently traded at 88 cents on the dollar. [12]

ADVANTAGES/DISADVANTAGES

DISTRESSED SECURITIES INVESTMENT strategies are event driven. Thus, they can provide opportunities in almost any economic environment because investment returns are dependent on specific corporate events rather than market conditions. Even during a recession or rising interest rate environment, a distressed security can perform well when the issuer reorganizes successfully. Because the strategy generates core returns based on events specific to the distressed company, such as bankruptcy filing, the outcome of intercreditor negotiations, or the amount of asset divestiture proceeds, its investment returns tend to have a low correlation to general financial markets.

However, investments in distressed securities are illiquid, which means that they do not lend themselves well to annual or more frequent liquidity windows. The length of any particular bankruptcy proceeding is notoriously hard to forecast and the outcome is always uncertain, both of which make the maturity of any particular investment in a distressed situation unpredictable. The prices of distressed securities are volatile during the bankruptcy process because useful information on the company becomes unavailable during this period. Investment managers who participate on creditor and equity committees must commit a large amount of time and must freeze their holdings until an arrangement is reached. Finally, distressed security specialists need to find defaulted securities of companies that have strong core operations.

PERFORMANCE

FROM JANUARY 1990 to March 1998, distressed securities strategies averaged an annualized rate of return of 19.64 percent with an average annual standard deviation of 5.66 percent. As could be expected, the recession years, 1990 and 1994, were off years for distressed specialists with returns of 6.43 and 3.84 percent. The recessions led to a number of good companies running into financial difficulties, which meant that there were ample distressed opportunities in the years that followed 1990 and 1994. These figures are evidence of the cyclical nature of distressed investing. In addition, the event-driven nature of distressed investing is made obvious by a correlation statistic of 0.0963, which means that changes in the prices of

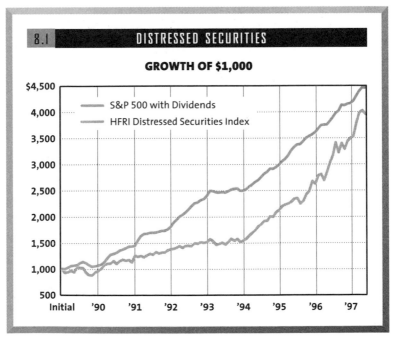

8.1 — DISTRESSED SECURITIES

GROWTH OF $1,000

S&P 500 with Dividends

HFRI Distressed Securities Index

the market as a whole have little effect on distressed invest-ing returns *(see Appendix C for updated performance)*.

SUMMARY POINTS

PROFIT OPPORTUNITY

◆ Distressed securities specialists invest in the securities of companies that are experiencing financial or operational difficulties.

◆ Because regulatory or policy constraints prevent many traditional investors from owning bankrupt or near-bankrupt companies, the securities of these companies are often priced significantly below distressed securities specialists' estimates of their "real" value.

◆ Distressed securities investment strategies are event driven, which means they provide opportunities in almost any economic environment because investment returns are dependent on specific corporate events rather than market conditions.

SOURCE OF RETURN

◆ Distressed securities specialists make investment returns on two kinds of mispricings: the fundamental value of securities and their value relative to the distressed company's other debt instruments.

◆ Distressed securities specialists combine financial analysis of the fundamental value of distressed companies with specialized knowledge of the bankruptcy process that allows them to predict, and when necessary take steps to influence, the outcome of bankruptcies and reorganizations.

INVESTMENT PROCESS

◆ Distressed securities specialists identify companies with strong operations that are overleveraged (good operating companies with excessive debt). They buy those companies' securities at a discount to their intrinsic value and anticipate the timing and consequence of major events, or "exit catalyst," that will lead to higher valuations.

◆ Companies with otherwise successful business operations go into default for two reasons: bad capital structure and adverse outside events.

◆ When they design a new capital structure, bankrupt companies will usually convert debt into equity, lower the interest costs, and extend the maturity on the remaining debt.

◆ The later in the bankruptcy cycle that an investor takes a position in a distressed company, the more certain is the outcome of the restructuring process. Because there is less risk in the later stages, the returns are usually also lower.

◆ The expertise of distressed securities specialists allows them to forecast the outcome of specific restructurings and judge whether a given company's securities are overvalued or undervalued.

◆ The specialist who can add value by becoming the exit catalyst will play an active role if the value added outweighs the opportunity cost of becoming involved.

KEY TERMS

Distressed securities. The securities of companies that are experiencing financial or operational difficulties. Distressed situations include reorganizations, bankruptcies, distressed sales, and other corporate restructurings.

Exit catalyst. An event on the horizon that the distressed securities specialist expects to change the market's perception of (and therefore the value of) the distressed company.

Fundamental value. The intrinsic or "real" value of a security, which reflects both tangible and intangible company assets.

Liquidation. The sale of assets for cash, sometimes to pay off debt.

Overleveraged company. A company that has too large an amount of debt relative to its ability to service that debt.

Relative value. The value of a particular security relative to that of other similar or related instruments, such as the same company's other debt instruments.

Senior debt. A class of debt securities whose holders a company is obligated to pay off before the holders of its other securities, in the case of bankruptcy.

Servicing debt. Paying the interest and principal due to bondholders.

CHAPTER

Event-Driven
STRATEGIES

RACTITIONERS OF *event-driven investment strategies* invest in the outcomes of the significant events that occur during corporate life cycles, such as bankruptcies, financial restructurings, mergers, acquisitions, and the spin-off of a division or subsidiary. The uncertainty about the outcome of these events creates investment opportunities for a specialist who can correctly anticipate their resolution. Generally, these extraordinary corporate events fall into three categories: risk arbitrage opportunities, distressed securities situations, and special situations. Event-driven specialists will shift the majority weighting of their portfolios to reflect the corporate events that offer the best investment opportunities.

Proponents of event-driven investment strategies argue that by focusing on corporate events, rather than market direction, these strategies will produce more consistent returns through various market environments than traditional approaches that depend on general trends in market price levels. Because corporate events are cyclical in nature, the prevailing corporate event activity fluctuates over time. For example, there are more mergers during periods of economic expansion and more bankruptcies during economic downturns. Event-driven strategists use specialized knowledge of all the significant events in the corporate life cycle and the flexibility to invest in the outcomes of a variety of corporate events to extract investment profits from the mispricings caused by uncertainty about the outcomes of these events.

CORE STRATEGY

INVESTORS WHO USE event-driven investment strategies focus on the outcomes of the significant events that occur during a corporation's life cycle. Generally, these extraordinary corporate events fall into three categories: risk arbitrage opportunities, distressed securities situations, and special situations. Risk arbitrage situations include hostile takeovers, mergers, acquisitions, and liquidations *(for a complete description of risk arbitrage strategies, see Chapter 7)*. Distressed security situations include recapitalizations, bankruptcies, restructurings, and reorganizations *(for a complete description of distressed securities strategies, see Chapter 8)*. Special situations include spin-offs, 13-D filings, and situations in which a company's asset mix is being significantly changed, such as the sale of major assets or a large share repurchase.

They look for three elements in any investment situation. First, they seek a disparity between the current market value of an instrument and the value that they anticipate for it after the event is completed. Second, they look for a near-term event to act as a **CATALYST** that will change the market's perception of the company and therefore its valuation of the company's debt or equity instruments and assess how likely it is to become visible. Third, they estimate the amount of time that it will take the catalyst to become fully visible to investors and how long the market will take to correct the valuation disparity.

Significant corporate events create profit opportunities because the outcome of the proposed changes is uncertain. Investment managers must ask: Will the event be completed? What will the result be if it does occur? How long will the process take? What effect will the event have on the prices of the securities of the involved companies? After a corporate event is announced, the price of the securities of the involved company reflects the market's uncertainty about whether the event will be completed. Event-driven specialists will make profits by correctly anticipating the outcome of these events.

INVESTMENT PROCESS

BECAUSE THE OVERALL volume and composition of corporate events vary over time and fluctuate with market cycles, event-driven specialists will shift the type of corporate event in which their portfolios are concentrated to take advantage of the best opportunities for risk-adjusted returns. In periods following a recession, such as 1991 to 1992, when many good companies experience financial difficulties, distressed securities offer the best opportunities for returns. In periods characterized by excellent economic markets, such as 1996 to 1997, when merger activity was at an all-time high, there are more risk arbitrage opportunities that offer good returns. In periods when the market is relatively flat, event-driven specialists will concentrate on special situations because they offer the best returns in any conditions and the high systemic risk usually associated with them is offset by the flat market conditions.

For event-driven specialists, the investment process is triggered by the public announcement of an impending corporate event. The manager must be convinced that a significant corporate event will take place during a definable period of time. Rather than try to anticipate corporate events, a process that is extremely speculative, event-driven specialists analyze the possible outcomes of events once they are announced. Once a proposed event is announced, the market revalues the securities of the companies involved on the basis of how it perceives the proposed event and the possible outcomes. Event-driven specialists research situations by using industry contacts, the advice of legal and banking experts, information from the financial newswires and magazines, and previous experiences and expertise. They understand the complex legal, interpersonal, and strategic forces that may affect the event and the probabilities of different potential outcomes. If a careful evaluation of the event indicates a favorable risk/reward criteria, the position is taken. Suc-

cessful event-driven specialists can synthesize **FUNDA-
MENTAL VALUE ANALYSIS**, **EVENT ANALYSIS**, and **TIME
HORIZON ANALYSIS**.

RISK CONTROL

EVENT-DRIVEN SPECIALISTS try to predict the outcome
of events or determine that the probability of the outcome
is greater than the current prices of the involved instruments indicate. Because the manager can be wrong about
any single case, the portfolio is diversified among a number of positions to reduce the impact of any single position that does not work out as anticipated. Maximum limits are set for the amount invested in any one event. As
mentioned earlier, event-driven specialists also diversify
across types of events (risk arbitrage, distressed securities,
special situations), depending on market cycles. Leverage
is used conservatively. They may hedge against market risk
by purchasing index put options and short selling.

MANAGER EXAMPLE

IN 1995, THE LOEWEN GROUP was the fastest growing
funeral home consolidator. As a result, its stock was trading in the $40s. In November 1995, a jury in Mississippi
ruled that Loewen was to pay a $500 million cash award.
As a result, Loewen's stock traded down to the high $20s.
Loewen sought to appeal the decision, and on January 24,
1996, the Mississippi Supreme Court ordered Loewen to
post a $625 million bond to continue the appeal. Loewen
threatened to file for bankruptcy, and as a result its stock
plummeted down to the mid-teens.

The event-driven specialist determined that there were
three possible outcomes: Loewen settles out of court,
Loewen posts the bond and appeals the ruling, or Loewen
files for bankruptcy.

If Loewen settled, it would be for an amount considerably lower than the amount the jury proposed, and the
chance that it would have to file for bankruptcy would be
considerably reduced. In this scenario, the specialist esti-

mated Loewen's stock would return to the $27 to $30 range.

If Loewen posted the bond and appealed the ruling, it would have to receive lines of credit from its banks to post the required bond. By doing so, Loewen would significantly increase its debt without resolving the issue. If Loewen won the appeal, its stock would return to the $30 level, but the appeal could take several years. If the company lost the appeal, it would have to file for bankruptcy or be bought out. Again, the process could take several years. If Loewen settled in court, its stock would trade up to the mid-$20s based on its fundamentals.

If Loewen filed for bankruptcy, the specialist estimated that its stock would trade down to $12. Loewen might become a takeover candidate and then be bought out at a higher level.

After analyzing the potential outcomes of the announced event, the event-driven specialist purchased Loewen's stock in the low teens because he liked the risk/reward ratio.

On January 29, 1996, the company settled the dispute with an after-tax present value package of $85 million in cash and securities. The event-driven specialist purchased additional shares around $27 and sold the entire position in the low $30s. He had held the position for approximately thirty days.[13]

ADVANTAGES/DISADVANTAGES

BECAUSE EVENT-DRIVEN strategies are positioned to take advantage of the valuation disparities produced by corporate events, they are less dependent on overall stock market gains than traditional equity investment approaches. Opportunities for high risk-adjusted returns may be identified even in a flat or declining market. Because their returns are determined in part by the volume of corporate events, event-driven specialists think that more opportunities will be available to them than managers who specialize only in risk arbitrage or dis-

tressed securities and the events driving their positions
will be more diversified. These advantages depend on the
event-driven specialist's expertise in the various types of
corporate events. Specialized knowledge of the whole
range of corporate events is required because profits are
determined not only by the number of corporate events
but also by the manager's ability to identify and correctly
anticipate their outcome.

PERFORMANCE

FROM JANUARY 1990 to March 1998, event-driven strategies registered an average annualized return of 18.85 percent, with an annualized standard deviation of 5.88. These
returns were slightly higher than the Standard and Poor's
500 index of blue-chip stocks for the same period of time,
with a much lower standard deviation (5.88 compared
with slightly more than 12). Event-driven funds registered
only 6 percent returns in 1994 and lost 0.5 percent in
1990, but in every other year between 1990 and 1997 they
registered returns between 19.47 percent and 28.23 per-

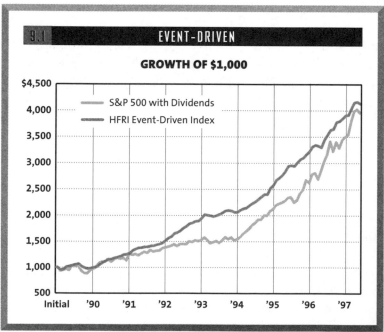

9.1   EVENT-DRIVEN

GROWTH OF $1,000

cent. Because the strategy capitalizes on corporate events, the event-driven index's correlation statistic of 0.3494 showed little sensitivity to the movement of stock prices in general *(see Appendix C for updated performance).*

SUMMARY POINTS

PROFIT OPPORTUNITY

◆ Event-driven strategists use specialized knowledge of all the significant events in the corporate life cycle and the flexibility to invest in the outcomes of a variety of corporate events to extract investment profits from the mispricings caused by uncertainty about the outcomes of significant corporate events.

◆ Generally, these extraordinary corporate events fall into three categories: risk arbitrage opportunities, distressed securities situations, and special situations.

◆ Event-driven specialists invest in situations in which they expect a near-term event to act as a catalyst that will change the market's perception of the company and therefore its valuation of the company's debt or equity instruments.

SOURCE OF RETURN

◆ Significant corporate events create profit opportunities because the outcome of the proposed changes is uncertain.

◆ Profits are made by correctly anticipating the outcome of these events once they are announced and how that outcome will affect the valuation of the company's debt or equity instruments.

◆ Because event-driven strategies are positioned to take advantage of the valuation disparities produced by corporate events, they are less dependent on overall stock market gains than traditional equity investment approaches.

INVESTMENT PROCESS

◆ Because the overall volume and composition of corporate events vary over time and fluctuate with market cycles, event-driven specialists will shift the majority weighting of their portfolios to take advantage of the different opportunities available during different parts of the business cycle.

◆ Successful event-driven specialists can synthesize fundamental value analysis, event analysis, and time horizon analysis.

◆ An event-driven specialist must have specialized knowledge of a broad range of corporate events because profits are determined not only by the number of corporate events, but also on the ability to identify and correctly anticipate their outcome.

KEY TERMS

Catalyst. A near-term event, such as a press release or a new product launch, that will heighten investor interest in or change the market's perception of a company.

Event analysis. The process by which an analyst assesses the probabilities of all the possible outcomes of a corporate event.

Fundamental value analysis. The process by which an analyst establishes a theoretical value of a company from an examination of its financial statements, operational history and forecasts, business climate, etc.

Significant corporate events. Major public events, such as mergers, bankruptcies, and spin-offs, that have the potential to dramatically change a company's makeup and as a result the valuation of its debt and equity instruments.

Spread. The valuation disparity between two related financial instruments caused by uncertainty about the outcome of a corporate event.

Time horizon analysis. The examination of the time frame for completion of a corporate event (if the event is going to happen, then when will it occur?).

CHAPTER

10

Macro
INVESTING

ACRO INVESTORS generate profits by identifying extreme price-value disparity and persistent trends in stock markets, interest rates, foreign exchange rates, and physical commodities and making leveraged bets on the price movements that they anticipate in these markets. To identify these extreme pricing disparities, they use a top-down global approach that concentrates on forecasting how global macroeconomic and political events affect the valuations of financial instruments. They have the broadest investment mandate of any of the hedge fund strategies, with the ability to hold positions in practically any market with any instrument. Macro investors make profits by correctly anticipating price movements in global markets and having the flexibility to use any investment approach that allows them to take advantage of extreme price dislocations. They may use a focused approach or diversify across various investments. Often, they will pursue a number of the other hedge fund strategies while waiting to take their selective large directional bets.

Perhaps it is because macro managers are the largest participants in the hedge fund industry and often receive the most attention in the press that a large portion of the investment community likes to see them as simply top-down analysts: speculators who try to make profits on currency, commodity, bond, and stock movements without researching specific companies and financial instruments. However, some macro managers argue that macro trends and conditions apply to micro investment approaches that are not normally considered "macro." They believe that specialist strategies such as risk arbitraging; investing in distressed securities, sectors, and emerging markets; and short selling are each successful in particular macro environments and not others. A large directional bet may be warranted when extraordinary sets of macro conditions create an extreme price disparity or a persistent trend that makes a particular investment approach very effective. In addition, many specialist strategies are difficult for managers in charge of huge amounts of assets. Some macro managers, such as George Soros and Julian Robertson, manage many billions of dollars in assets. Macro managers are able to take advantage of the opportunities produced by extraordinary sets of macro conditions because they have the flexibility to move large amounts of capital into a variety of different investment positions in a timely fashion.

It may seem that macro strategies have nothing in common with the other hedge fund strategies, but that is because it is a general approach rather than a specialized approach. Although the differences are certainly obvious, the similarities are more important for the purposes of this book. Like the other hedge fund strategies, macro investing leverages a strategic advantage and the flexibility to move from opportunity to opportunity, without restriction, to extract investment returns from market inefficiencies that cannot always be accessed by traditional investment approaches that are more restricted. George Soros once said of his style of investing, "I don't play the game by a particular set of rules; I look for changes in the rules of the game."[14]

CORE STRATEGY

MACRO INVESTORS LOOK for the extraordinary sets of macro conditions that occur only occasionally and that make a particular investment approach very effective while those conditions persist. They enjoy a great deal of investment policy flexibility and will therefore invest on a leveraged base across multiple sectors, markets, instruments, and trading styles as the macro conditions dictate. They invest based on macroeconomic analysis and forecasts of changes in interest rates, currency markets, equity markets, and global political and economic policy. They often pursue other hedge fund strategy while waiting to take the large, opportunistic directional positions for which they are more famous. Generally, macro investors look for unusual price fluctuations. They refer to such extremes as far-from-equilibrium conditions. In such situations, market participants' perceptions and the actual state of affairs are very far removed from one another and create a persistent price trend. The macro investor makes profits by identifying where in the economy the risk premium has swung farthest from equilibrium, investing in that situation, and recognizing when the extraordinary conditions that made that particular approach so profitable have deteriorated or have been counteracted by a new trend in the opposite direction. For the macro investor, timing is everything.

INVESTMENT PROCESS

THINK OF PRICES as falling on a bell curve. Macro investors argue that most price fluctuations in financial markets fall within one standard deviation of the mean. They consider this volatility to be the ordinary state of affairs, which does not offer particularly good investment opportunities. However, when price fluctuations of particular instruments or markets push out more than two standard deviations from the mean into the tails of the bell curve, an extreme condition occurs that may only appear once every two or three decades. As discussed in previous chapters, when market prices differ from the "real" value of an asset, there exists an arbitrage opportunity. The macro investor makes profits by arbitraging such extreme price/value valuations back to normal levels. Some examples of far-from-equilibrium conditions that have occurred in recent years are junk bonds and emerging-market debt in the early 1990s, Eurodollars in 1994, and the Japanese yen during the late 1980s and again recently.

Perhaps the most famous formulation of the macro theory of investing is George Soros's boom-bust sequence. The sequence begins with an initial phase in which a prevailing macro trend becomes joined with a prevailing investor bias so that the two reinforce each other. If the trend can withstand external shocks such as a policy pronouncement and emerges strengthened, then it is in a period of acceleration. The moment of truth happens when market beliefs diverge from reality so much that their bias becomes recognized as a bias. This is followed by a twilight period, in which the trend is sustained by inertia but ceases to be reinforced by market participants and so flattens out. At some point (the inflection point), this loss of faith causes a reversal in the trend, which had become dependent on an ever-stronger bias. The inflection point is usually marked or signaled by a major policy move, which then precipitates the crash, in which the market bias in the opposite direction of the original trend accelerates the return to normalcy. The art of macro investing lies in determining when a process has been stretched to its inflection point and when to become involved in its trend back to equilibrium.

MANAGER EXAMPLE

IN THE MID-1980s, Japan had a very high savings rate, a strong currency, extremely low inflation and interest rates, and a very high-priced stock market, which allowed Japanese companies to raise capital at a very low cost. At the same time, the Japanese have a limited supply of land. In the mid-1980s, there was a housing shortage, and the cost of housing went up much faster than wages. Because of this state of affairs, the Japanese saved even more to be able to purchase houses. The flaw in the process was that it exacerbated the difference between those who owned houses and those who did not. This divisive social force led to a political upheaval. The Ministry of Finance propped up the economy for a couple of years, but eventually a stage was reached when Japanese banks had to be paid to take a deposit. The Japanese started buying bonds in the United States, a trend that reinforced itself because of the desperate need for the yen to depreciate. Finally, under pressure from long-term trade surpluses that created an endless demand for yen, the stock market and the real estate markets collapsed. This created a vicious cycle of repatriation of capital from abroad and a far-from-equilibrium valuation of the yen.

Most macro investors perceived that the yen was overvalued in the mid- to late 1980s, but not all of them were able to make profits from this valuation extreme. Many, including Soros, entered the market prematurely and suffered heavy losses. In 1987, Soros was long U.S. stocks and short Japanese stocks in anticipation of the forthcoming bust and correction. However, the bust came in the United States first and not in Japan for another two years. The art of macro investing is not always in identifying extreme overvaluations. Rather, it is in identifying when and where the inflection point or policy response has occurred that will trigger the subsequent reversal of the trend.[15]

ADVANTAGES/DISADVANTAGES

MACRO INVESTORS ARE not confined by a market niche, enjoying the flexibility and objectivity to move from opportunity to opportunity and trend to trend. This is particularly important because macro investors' asset size per fund is the largest in the hedge fund industry. Potentially asset size can hinder the execution of strategy, but macro investing makes asset size an advantage rather than a hindrance. Macro investing is often portrayed as risky directional betting or speculating. This view is reinforced by the large profits and losses that these funds generate when concentrated leveraged bets pay off—or fail.

PERFORMANCE

FROM JANUARY 1990 to March 1998, macro hedge funds recorded an average annualized return of 23.09 percent, with an annualized standard deviation of 9.39. These returns were nearly 5 percent more than the Standard and Poor's 500 index of blue-chip stocks recorded for the same period of time, with lower volatility. In 1991 and

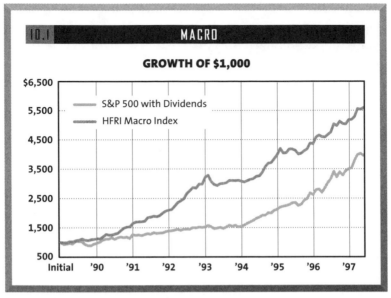

10.1 **MACRO**

GROWTH OF $1,000

Legend: S&P 500 with Dividends; HFRI Macro Index

X-axis: Initial, '90, '91, '92, '93, '94, '95, '96, '97
Y-axis: 500, 1,500, 2,500, 3,500, 4,500, 5,500, $6,500

1993, macro funds registered returns of 46.70 and 53.30 percent. In 1992 and 1995, they returned 27.16 and 29.30 percent. Other than 1994, when they recorded a loss of 4.31 percent, macro funds exhibited consistently high performance, with a .2511 correlation to general stock market price changes *(see Appendix C for updated performance)*.

SUMMARY POINTS

PROFIT OPPORTUNITY

◆ Macro managers are able take advantage of the extreme price valuations produced by extraordinary sets of macro conditions because they have the flexibility to move large amounts of capital into a variety of different investment positions in a timely fashion.

◆ Macro investors look for the extraordinary sets of macro conditions that occur only occasionally and that make a particular investment approach very effective while those conditions persist.

◆ Macro managers represent a small percentage of existing hedge funds, but individual macro managers have the largest asset size under management in the industry.

SOURCE OF RETURN

◆ Macro investors make profits by identifying where in the economy the risk premium has swung farthest from equilibrium, investing in that situation, and recognizing when the extraordinary conditions that made that particular approach so profitable have deteriorated or been counteracted by a new trend in the opposite direction.

INVESTMENT PROCESS

◆ The art of macro investing is determining when a process has been stretched to its inflection point and when to become involved in its trend back to normalcy.

◆ Macro investors enjoy the flexibility and objectivity to move from opportunity to opportunity and trend to trend.

KEY TERMS

Arbitrage. The simultaneous purchase and sale of a security or pair of similar securities to profit from a pricing discrepancy.

Boom-bust sequence. The process by which the value of an instrument or class of instruments is pushed to a valuation extreme, reverses itself, and crashes back to a more normal valuation.

Far-from-equilibrium condition. An unusual macro situation characterized by persistent price trends or extreme price valuations of particular financial instruments.

Inflection point. The point at which an extreme valuation reverses itself, usually marked or signaled by a major policy move.

Speculator. An investor who makes large directional bets on what financial markets will do next.

CHAPTER

Sector
FUNDS

ECTOR SPECIALISTS confine their investment universe to a specific industry, segment of the economy, or other grouping that shares a common product, market, or theme. They can invest long and short in various instruments and diversify their portfolios across either the entire sector or some subsector. The managers of sector funds combine fundamental financial analysis with industry expertise to identify the best profit opportunities in the sector. The opportunities that they identify are not necessarily growth stocks. In a down market, they may make profits by identifying the worst-performing stocks in the sector. They will sometimes hedge against market or sector price declines through the purchase of index put options or selling short overvalued stocks.

Sector funds engage in one or more of the hedge fund strategies but limit their investment universe to a specific industry or other concentration.

Although this strategy is categorized by the specific investment universe rather than investment activities and return source, most pursue equity hedge or event-driven approaches.

CORE STRATEGY

INVESTMENT MANAGERS WHO specialize in particular SECTORS or industries often invest in the sectors of the economy with long-term growth rates superior to the market in general. Many hold primarily long core positions in the companies that offer the best value in those industries. By investing in sectors with superior growth rates, these managers increase their chances of identifying top-performing stocks. However, many sector hedge fund managers do not have such a bias toward their sector. They can profit in down markets by using their specialized knowledge, experience, and the flexibility to sell short the stocks of the worst companies, especially those also in the weakest sectors, and earn profit accordingly. In recent years, the most prominent and successful sector funds have been concentrated in the biomedical, health care, energy, information technology, media, and financial industries. Often, sector specialists are former or present participants in the industry in which they invest and can draw on industry expertise and industry contacts to which investors with a more general approach do not have access. In addition, they often count among their clients experts and current participants in the particular industry who are fluent in its processes and associated technologies. The sector fund formula is a simple one: combine fundamental financial analysis with industry expertise to create an informational advantage that allows the sector specialist to identify the best profit opportunities.

ONE MANAGER'S LOGIC OF SECTORS

SECTOR SPECIALISTS USUALLY look for at least two of the following three things in a sector: **1** high growth rates relative to the general market, **2** an industry in which the specialist holds a distinct informational advantage, and **3** the size and breadth to offer plentiful opportunities that are independently affected by a variety of factors.

One has only to look at the biotech sector to have a full appreciation of the potential upside of sector funds. The AMEX biotech index is down 55 percent from seven years ago; yet the Dow Jones Industrial Average is up over 275 percent during the same period.

Why is it that the large pharmaceutical companies, such as Merck, Pfizer, and Johnson & Johnson, were up manyfold after the Clinton health care program failed? Why is it that companies such as Amgen and Genzyme—companies created over a decade ago with market values in the billions—are still the top-tiered biotech companies and have not been replaced by any of the other 500 publicly traded companies that were created in that time?

The answer is that these large pharmaceutical companies are revenue-producing companies and that most biotech companies, because of the lack of funding, have become royalty-based companies. The only capital available to them is from the large pharmaceutical companies, who in return for their $5 to $10 million, gain the rights and revenues of those biotech companies' late-stage products. Today, biotech companies have over 300 Phase III drugs going before the FDA in the near future, spend $7.5 billion annually in research, and have a combined market capitalization of only $75 billion. This compares to Merck, which alone has a market capitalization of $140 billion yet only 26 Phase III drugs and spends only $1.5 billion in research.

Today, sophisticated hedge funds can go both long and short, and pick from a variety of factors in order to achieve significant returns. They can review biotech companies based on their product line, cash on hand, competitive valuation with other companies in their sector, patent protection, etc. The reality is that there will be more and more multibillion-dollar drugs like Viagra in the coming years.

Over the next decade, there should be major breakthroughs in cancer, Alzheimer's, stroke, diabetes, and heart disease research. Lastly, there is no other sector in which investors can have more of a direct impact on the quality of life for their children and grandchildren.[16]

MANAGER EXAMPLE

FIRSTAR CORPORATION (FSR) is a $21 billion bank holding company headquartered in Milwaukee, Wisconsin. The bank has the largest Wisconsin banking franchise as well as operations elsewhere in surrounding states. FSR had been a well-performing company, but in the latter 1990s it experienced slower growth in earnings. Many analysts regarded it as a prime takeover candidate regardless of management's insistence on independence and even reaffirmation of its policy to acquire other banks.

In 1998, FSR's stock price declined from 42 in late February to 33 in late June, mainly because many "generalist" investors concluded that high takeover premiums would not be paid for large regional bank acquisitions; hence they sold out of positions that had been acquired in hopes of realizing big gains if the stocks were acquired. For investors who were very familiar with the bank merger market the sell-off was a golden opportunity to acquire stock cheaply in a highly prized banking franchise.

The real opportunity arrived, however, when it was announced on July 1 that StarBanc (STB) in Cincinnati had agreed to acquire FSR in an all-stock transaction equivalent to a 44 percent market premium based on prices prevailing before the merger was rumored to be happening in *The Wall Street Journal*. The agreed fixed exchange ratio with no collars meant that FSR would trade in tandem with STB and that, if the market liked the deal, FSR would appreciate even more (of course the downside risk was also present). STB management and many analysts believed the deal to be substantially accretive to STB earnings per share, to the tune of 12 to 14 percent in fiscal 1999. This high level of accretion is unusual in bank deals and implied that STB's stock price should rise by the same amount if the market is rational.

In fact, STB declined by 8 percent in trading immediately after the announcement. Opportunistic hedge funds that could recognize this huge disparity in value and move quickly enough seized on the opportunity to buy FSR, even after it was up nearly 40 percent in two days. After the market's knee-jerk reaction of selling off STB, smart buyers came into the market and within a few days drove STB up 17 percent from its preannouncement level, bringing FSR up over 50 percent from its prerumor price. At these levels, both stocks were fairly valued and the "icing on the cake" had been removed; thus, many opportunistic hedge fund investors sold and redeployed their capital. However, a good merger arbitrage position was created by many hedge funds, locking in a nonleveraged annualized return of 17 percent by owning FSR and shorting STB. This return was locked in so long as the deal closed by year-end 1998 and the terms of the deal remained unchanged. The FSR/STB transaction is a good example of how a specialized investor can benefit from patience, temporary irrational price behavior, and eventually appropriate stock pricing. [17]

INVESTMENT PROCESS

MANY SECTOR SPECIALISTS try to identify growth stocks with earnings and cash flow numbers that are selling at a significant discount to the company's intrinsic value. They also look for a catalytic event to heighten investor interest in the company. A catalytic event could be, among other things, a new product launch, a regulatory approval, or a corporate restructuring. The logic is reversed when sector specialists are looking for stocks to sell short. In that case, they look for overvalued stocks and a catalytic event to expose the company's weaknesses. In addition, sector specialists remain aware of macro economic, monetary, and cyclical elements that affect the overall level of the equity market and the position of their particular sector relative to that market. Before making an investment, many sector specialists meet with company management to get to know the people behind the numbers and to understand their business model. To understand the company's position in the industry, they also meet with customers, suppliers, employees, and competitors.

An equity hedge style sector specialist's portfolio usually has two components: core positions and trading and hedging positions. Core positions are long-term positions that are rarely turned over and are a key source of investment returns. The rest of the portfolio is composed of trading positions, short positions in overvalued companies, and hedging positions. These account for most of portfolio turnover and allow sector hedge fund managers to make profits in both up and down markets. They may sell long positions when a company changes management or they cease to understand its business model. If they invest in a company because of a specific economic event, they will usually sell after that event has taken place. In sum, long positions will be reconsidered if there is a change in the original investment rationale.

RISK CONTROL

SECTOR SPECIALISTS CONTROL risk by maintaining a balance between diversification and concentration in meaningful positions. If there are a variety of factors driving the sector that are independent of each other, the specialist will make investments that represent his or her understanding of the different factors so that different positions are not subject to the same fluctuations. Some sector specialists will also hedge their long positions with offsetting short positions or hedge the market by using index options. Another important risk consideration for sector specialists is investment time horizons. They try to align properly with the time horizons of companies in which they invest. If the manager invests in a company and the preferred investment horizon is shorter than that company's business plan warrants, the result is unintended volatility risks in the short term.

ADVANTAGES/DISADVANTAGES

SECTOR FUNDS CAN be attractive investments because most sector fund candidate companies benefit from being in a fast-growing industry or sector. Top-performing companies can produce extremely high returns, and even mediocre ones may generate desirable returns. In addition, sector specialists usually bring a great deal of experience and expertise to the process of unlocking the best profit opportunities on both the long and short sides in a sector.

The sector portfolio allows investors to do their own diversification. If investors use sector funds as a component of a larger portfolio, they can decide how much to allocate to any given sector. More important, they can choose the manager for each sector who best matches their risk/reward requirements. Although generalists can be very successful, for many sectors a specialist may be better able to navigate the often complex businesses and available investment opportunities in that sector. Because they have a finite list of investment options, sector specialists have more time to examine industry details and build relationships with industry contacts and company management.

The limited focus of a sector fund can be seen as both an advantage and a disadvantage. A small sector provides relatively few investment options. In addition, because companies within a sector may be affected by related events, their investment returns may be highly correlated. If the entire sector takes a downturn, the sector specialist will often fall with it. The fortunes of a sector specialist often depend on technology life cycles and the caprices of product development. As a result, sector specialists must accept short-term portfolio volatility and sometimes find it difficult to sufficiently diversify their holdings. However, the limited universe of stocks in which they navigate means they can gain a more intimate knowledge of the industry. In larger sectors, managers can diversify across the many subsectors. The preponderance of subsectors makes it somewhat difficult to compare sector hedge fund managers in the traditional ways, so merely comparing the results of managers dealing in the same broad group of stocks is not always enough. A good comparison also takes into account the investment style of the managers and the use of leverage and hedging positions.

PERFORMANCE

FROM JANUARY 1990 through March 1998, the Hedge Fund Research, Inc. composite index of sector hedge funds recorded an average annualized return of 26.23 percent, the highest average annualized return of any of the hedge fund strategies over the same period of time. Furthermore, the annual standard deviation of 9.17 was sig-

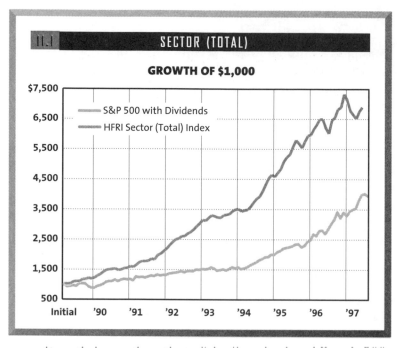

11.1   SECTOR (TOTAL)

GROWTH OF $1,000

- S&P 500 with Dividends
- HFRI Sector (Total) Index

niticantly lower than that of the Standard and Poor's 500. However, it is no more useful to evaluate all sector funds as a group than it is to combine the diverse hedge funds strategies. Therefore, this chapter breaks down these performance figures into funds that are operating in some of the more prominent sectors. From January 1992 through March 1998, hedge funds specializing in the financial sector averaged 32.11 percent returns, with an annual standard deviation of 8.25. They recorded a high of 49.35 in 1997 and a low of 11.12 in 1994. From January 1993 to March 1998, hedge funds specializing in health care and biotechnology averaged 18.85 percent returns, with an annual standard deviation of 14.30. This included a 10.35 percent loss in 1994 and 67.58 percent gain in 1995. From January 1991 to March 1998, hedge funds specializing in technology averaged 24.74 percent, with an annual standard deviation of 14.32. These returns included a 50.91 percent gain in 1995 and a low return of 6.89 percent in 1997. The figures for these different sectors expose some of the problems with defining the general principles of a sector strategy. Two points, mentioned earlier, must be emphasized: the logic changes from sector to sector, and these performance figures tell the story of sectors in only the most general way *(see Appendix C for updated performance)*.

SUMMARY POINTS

PROFIT OPPORTUNITY

◆ Sector specialists look for at least two of the following three things in a sector: high growth rates relative to the general market, an industry in which the specialist holds a distinct informational advantage, and the size and breadth to offer plentiful opportunities that are independently affected by a variety of factors.

◆ By investing in a sector that is outgrowing other sectors, managers can increase their chances of identifying top-performing stocks. Most companies benefit from being in a fast-growing industry. The top-performing companies can produce extremely high returns, whereas even mediocre ones may generate desirable returns.

◆ Sector specialists may sell short to hedge or profit in down markets.

◆ The sector portfolio allows investors to handle their own diversification.

◆ A sector fund's limited focus can be seen as an advantage and a disadvantage. A small sector provides relatively few investment options, but the specialist gains an intimate knowledge of that universe of stocks.

SOURCE OF RETURN

◆ The sector fund formula is a simple one: combine fundamental financial analysis with industry expertise to create an informational advantage that allows the sector specialist to identify the best profit opportunities in the sector.

◆ An equity hedge style sector specialist's portfolio usually has two components: core positions and trading and hedging positions. Core positions are long-term positions that are rarely turned over and are a key source of investment returns. The rest of the portfolio will be made up of trading positions: short positions in overvalued companies and hedging positions that account for most of the portfolio's turnover and allow sector hedge fund managers to make profits in both up and down markets.

INVESTMENT PROCESS

◆ Sector specialists identify growth stocks with earnings and cash flow numbers that are selling at a significant discount to the company's intrinsic value.

◆ Sector specialists also look for a catalytic event that will heighten investor interest in the company, and thus reduce the current discount to intrinsic value.

KEY TERMS

Catalytic event. A near-term event, such as a new product launch, that heightens investor interest in a company.

Core positions. Long-term positions in growth stocks from which managers derive the majority of their profits.

Growth stock. A stock that an investor believes will appreciate because the company's output and earnings will grow.

Hedging. The taking of positions to offset changes in economic conditions falling outside the core investment idea, such as the purchase of index options to offset changes in the overall level of the equity market.

Sector. A group of companies or segment of the economy that is similar in either its product or its market, for example, health care, biotechnology, financial services, or information technologies.

Trading positions. Opportunistic positions designed to take advantage of short-term market mispricings and inefficiencies.

CHAPTER 12

Equity
HEDGE

EQUITY HEDGE STRATEGISTS combine core long holdings of equities with short sales of stock or stock index options. Their portfolios may be anywhere from net long to net short, depending on market conditions. They increase long exposure in bull markets and decrease it or even go net short in a bear market. Generally, the short exposure is intended to generate an ongoing positive return in addition to acting as a hedge against a general stock market decline. In a rising market, equity hedge strategists expect their long holdings to appreciate more than the market and their short holdings to appreciate less than the market. Similarly, in a declining market, they expect their short holdings to fall more rapidly than the market falls and their long holdings to fall less rapidly than the market. The idea is to take long positions in stocks that will outperform the market and sell short stocks that will underperform

the market. The source of return for equity hedge
fund managers is similar to that of traditional stock
pickers on the upside, but differs in the use of short
selling and hedging to outperform the market on the
downside.

Of all the hedge fund strategies, equity hedge
strategies have the longest name lineage. They are a
direct descendent of A. W. Jones's original "hedge"
fund. However, as was the case in the initial hedge
fund rush of the late 1960s, during the bull market of
the 1990s many practitioners have foregone the **SHORT
EXPOSURE** that was characteristic of the original funds.
Thus, the present incarnations of the strategy can be
roughly divided into two groups: equity hedge and
equity nonhedge. The equity hedge strategists who
are true to the original formulation retain the old
structure that combined a core leveraged long stock
position with a short exposure that protects against

downside risk. Equity nonhedge strategists use a strategy similar to traditional long-only strategies but with the freedom to use varying amounts of leverage. Although most of them reserve the right to sell short, short sales are not an ongoing component of their investment portfolios, and many have not carried short positions at all. This chapter discusses equity nonhedge as a variation of the equity hedge strategy. At heart, these are both concentrated stock-picking strategies, one that hedges market risk by augmenting core long positions with short positions, and the other that forgoes that short exposure. The freedom to use leverage, take short positions, and hedge long positions is a strategic advantage that differentiates equity hedge strategists from traditional long-only equity investors.

CORE STRATEGY

EQUITY HEDGE STRATEGISTS combine core long holdings with short sales of stock or stock index options. Investors sell stock short if they expect the price of the stock to decline. To sell a stock short, an investor borrows that stock and immediately sells it on the market with the intention of buying it back later at a lower price and returning it to the lender. If the price of the stock declines, then the investor makes profits on the difference between the selling price and the cost of the replacement stock. The cash proceeds from the sale are held in a money market account, earning interest. Equity hedge strategists maintain a basket of shorted stocks as a hedge against a drop in the overall market. To the degree that they match their long holdings with short positions, the matched portion of the portfolio may be called **WITHIN THE HEDGE**. In theory, the long positions will generate profits in a rising market, and short positions will generate profits in a declining one. Therefore, for the long and short positions within the hedge, the fund manager has eliminated any systemic risk associated with the market as a whole and shifted the emphasis to the ability to pick stocks. In a rising market, equity hedge strategists expect their long holdings to appreciate more than the market and their short holdings to appreciate less than the market. Similarly, in a declining market, they expect their short positions to fall more rapidly than the market falls and their long holdings to fall less rapidly than the market. The idea is to take long positions in stocks that will outperform the market and sell short stocks that will underperform the market.

When investors borrow funds to increase the amount they have invested in a particular stock position, they are using **LEVERAGE**. Investors use leverage when they believe that the return from the stock position will exceed the cost of the borrowed funds. Investors who use leverage increase the risk of their investment; therefore, they usually try to only use it in extremely low-risk situations. Most equity hedge strategists use leverage. Leverage allows them to add new stocks to the portfolio without waiting to sell something else off first. Aggressive equity hedge managers will use leverage to move quickly to exploit investment opportunities. More conservative equity hedge managers will use leverage more sparingly, but the deployment of some amount of leverage is a characteristic of equity hedge funds in general.

Equity hedge specialists are aware that the prices of individual stocks can, and often do, move in response to factors unrelated to the direction of the overall market. Thus, if they pick their stocks well, it is entirely possible for equity hedge managers to make money on both long positions and short positions on the same day. Theoretically, they can make money in both up and down markets because they retain the flexibility to go both long and short. Equity hedge fund managers' source of return is similar to that of traditional stock pickers on the upside, but they use short selling and hedging to outperform the market on the downside. Although equity hedge portfolios may not outperform a traditional long-only stock portfolio in a bull market, over time they should outperform the stock market on a risk-adjusted basis because they will outperform the stock market in down and sideways markets.

INVESTMENT PROCESS

EQUITY HEDGE STRATEGISTS will adjust their **NET MAR-KET EXPOSURE** as market conditions warrant. In a bull market, they will try to be net long. In a bear market, they will try to have less market exposure, possibly going net short. A simplified version of the formula that they use to calculate market exposure is shown below:

$$\text{Market exposure} = \frac{\text{Long exposure} - \text{Short exposure}}{\text{Capital}}$$

For example, if a fund manager had $1,000,000 in capital to invest and borrowed a further $500,000, then if he or she took long positions worth $900,000 and short positions worth $600,000, the net market exposure would be 300,000/1,000,000, or 30 percent net long. Conservative fund managers will mitigate risk by keeping market exposure between 0 and 100 percent. More aggressive funds may magnify risk by exceeding 100 percent exposure or, alternatively, by maintaining a net short exposure. Some fund managers prefer to concentrate on stock picking and thus will pay little or no attention to macro trends. The aggregate market exposure of their portfolios will depend on whether they are finding better investment opportunities on the long or the short side. These managers take short positions primarily as opportunities to make investment returns, rather than merely to hedge against market decline. This is usually called a **TRADING POSITION** as opposed to a hedging position. Although almost all equity hedge managers vary the long/short relationship in their portfolios, it is important to take note of whether market exposure is a result of hedging or trading positions.

Equity hedge strategists generate investment ideas by reading newspapers and trade journals, talking to clients and partners, attending conferences and road shows, and keeping in constant contact with industry experts. They narrow their focus to the companies with the best fundamental outlook, the best dynamic within a group of related companies, and the best investment potential on the individual level. Before allocating any capital to an idea, most equity hedge managers make site visits to assess the energy, ability, and commitment of the company's management and speak with competitors, suppliers, and customers to verify the company's position within its industry. They attempt to be early in identifying economic trends that will have a major impact on the market. As with any other investment strategy, investment ideas that are not yet widely known are the best ideas. In addition, they seek an identifiable catalyst that will focus the investment community's attention on the company, such as better-than-expected earnings or positive press releases. What does this mean for stock pickers? It means they must look hard at businesses to judge what it will take for them to succeed in the future, and identify which company has the most of it. In different industries, this could mean different things. It might be product development in one industry and marketing in another. In any case, equity hedge strategists look for the companies that have a competitive advantage that will enable them to capitalize on an important economic trend and take long core positions in those companies.

MANAGER EXAMPLE

DELL COMPUTER CORPORATION was our largest gain on the long side during the first quarter of 1998. Throughout our long-term ownership of Dell, the company has further expanded its market share through flawless execution of its direct-sales strategy. Several of its competitors have paid Dell the highest form of compliment by attempting to shift to the direct-sales, build-to-order strategy so effectively utilized by Dell. These competitors risked the stability of their traditional reseller channels trying to pursue Dell. While we believed it would take several years for the negative impact on the reseller channel to unfold, Compaq recently announced that they would not meet investor expectations in the first quarter due in part to problems involving reseller channel inventories. There is more to the success of Dell Computer than merely utilizing a build-to-order sales model. Dell continues to leverage its direct-selling strategy to improve the returns generated on its invested capital by virtually integrating its customer and supplier relationships. This seamless integration yields enormous operating leverage that is used to drive increasing returns on a decreasing working-capital base.[18]

MANAGER EXAMPLE

BACK IN MID-1994, we were introduced to a small company named WinStar Communications, which had accumulated a large amount of 38-gigahertz radio spectrum for use as a wireless alternative to traditional local phone service. The opportunity was huge: the local voice and data networks, with $90 billion of annual revenues, were controlled by the monopolist Baby Bells, but deregulation was sure to come, just as it had to the long-distance business once dominated by AT&T. Furthermore, the Baby Bells' infrastructure was geared toward carrying voice traffic rather than data, and they were having a hard time keeping up with the demand for high-capacity connections. A number of small competitors known as CLECs (competitive local exchange carriers) had begun building their own fiber-optic networks to provide specialized services to businesses. However, laying fiber-optic cable was too costly for many applications. WinStar felt strongly that there would be a large potential market for a "wireless fiber" service. They hired a team of industry veterans, including some of the key people involved with the early growth of MCI and Sprint, and rapidly put their plan into action. The stock became a huge winner, up roughly six times since our first purchases. The CLEC group turned red hot, driven by the exponential growth in data traffic because of the Internet, and by the increased merger and acquisition activity in the telecom industry after the enactment of the Telecommunications Reform Act of 1996. AT&T later bought Teleport, a leading CLEC (with hybrid fiber and 38-gigahertz network), for close to $10 billion: using comparable valuation measures, WinStar would be worth roughly $100 per share; the stock is currently around $30.[19]

RISK CONTROL

EQUITY HEDGE STRATEGISTS expose themselves primarily to stock-picking risks. By doing fundamental, bottom-up research on the companies in which they invest, equity hedge managers try to avoid the disastrous state of affairs of having their long positions dropping while their short positions are rising. For those managers who carefully adjust their long and short exposures as the market dictates, there is the risk of getting caught too net long in a market decline or too net short in a market rally. Although the portion of an equity hedge portfolio that is "within the hedge" may approximate market neutrality, at any given time managers can lose money on both their long and short positions. The portion of the portfolio that is not hedged is, of course, susceptible to all the various caprices of the market. The equity hedge manager will hedge as many of these risks as possible with specific hedging positions. He or she may hedge against exposure to a specific industry by "pair trading." When managers trade in pairs, they go long a stock in a particular industry and short a stock in the same industry, so that in the case of a systemic drop in the prices of the industry as a whole, the long and short positions offset each other. In addition, equity hedge managers will diversify their portfolios across industries and sectors to ensure that happenings in any one industry do not have too much effect on the portfolio as a whole.

Many equity hedge strategists use position limits to control the impact that any one position can have on the portfolio as a whole. If a position grows in market value and becomes a larger weighting in the portfolio, then they may trim it back. They will sell those stocks that reach their target valuations or those for which they lose con-

viction about the underlying growth qualities that origi-
nally prompted the position. When the price of a stock
does not behave as expected, the manager reassesses the
position. Generally, equity hedge managers are more tol-
erant of unexpected price moves in core holdings than in
trading positions.

ADVANTAGES/DISADVANTAGES

THE MAJOR ADVANTAGE of an equity hedge strategy is the
ability to hold both long and short positions. This gives the
strategy an ability to generate returns in both up and down
markets. Proponents will argue that nobody knows exactly
where the market is going next or why. Therefore, they will
give up a certain amount of the upside to soften the blow
of down markets. Equity hedge funds can generate returns
that are similar to traditional long-only, stock-picking
investment vehicles but with less volatility and less market
exposure because of the short exposure. Equity hedge
funds can generate returns that do not fluctuate as vio-
lently as traditional long-only funds. There is, of course,
no guarantee that equity hedge managers will be able to
achieve this. No matter how hedged, this strategy requires

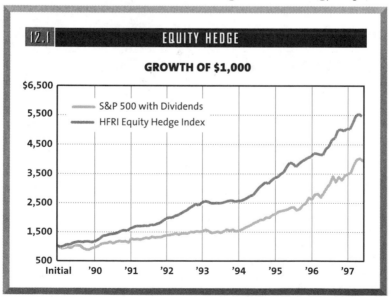

12.1 **EQUITY HEDGE**

GROWTH OF $1,000

a manager who can pick stocks well and correctly manage the long/short mix.

The bull market has enticed many equity hedge managers to forego any short exposure in favor of leveraged long-only positions. Bear markets have historically punished those managers who do so. To succeed over time, equity hedge managers must retain the discipline to match market exposure to market conditions.

PERFORMANCE

FROM JANUARY 1990 to March 1998, equity hedge funds registered average annualized returns of 22.86 percent, with an annualized standard deviation of 7.45. For the same period, equity nonhedge funds registered average annualized returns of 22.10, with an annualized standard deviation of 12.47. Both groups had higher returns than the Standard and Poor's 500 index of blue-chip stocks, and equity hedge funds did so with much less volatility. The downside protection characteristic of equity hedge funds made for slightly lower returns than equity nonhedge funds in the rising stock markets of 1991, 1995, and 1996 but more than made up for it in the falling market in

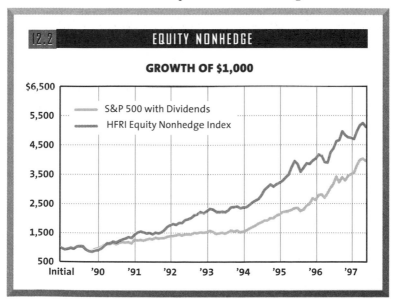

12.2 EQUITY NONHEDGE

GROWTH OF $1,000

S&P 500 with Dividends
HFRI Equity Nonhedge Index

1990, with 14.42 percent returns compared with 7.17 for equity nonhedge funds. Equity hedge fund returns are less sensitive to price changes in the overall stock market than equity nonhedge, as evidenced by a correlation statistic of 0.3286 as compared with 0.7573 *(see Appendix C for updated performance)*.

SUMMARY POINTS

PROFIT OPPORTUNITY

◆ The flexibility to use leverage, take short positions, and hedge long positions is a strategic advantage that differentiates equity hedge strategists from traditional long-only equity investors.

◆ Equity hedge strategists combine core long holdings with short sales of stock or stock index options. They maintain a basket of shorted stocks as a hedge against a drop in the overall market.

◆ By having equal amounts of long and short positions within the hedge, the fund manager has eliminated any systemic risk associated with the market as a whole and shifted the emphasis to his or her ability to pick stocks.

SOURCE OF RETURN

◆ Aggressive equity hedge managers will use leverage to move quickly to exploit investment opportunities. More conservative equity hedge managers will use leverage more sparingly, but the deployment of some amount of leverage is a characteristic of equity hedge funds in general.

◆ Theoretically, equity hedge specialists can make money in both up and down markets because they retain the flexibility to go both long and short.

◆ Although equity hedge portfolios may not outperform a traditional long-only stock portfolio in a bull market, over time, they should outperform the stock market on a risk-adjusted basis because they should outperform the stock market in down and sideways markets.

INVESTMENT PROCESS

◆ Equity hedge strategists will adjust their net market exposure as market conditions dictate. In a bull market, they will try to be net long. In a bear market, they will try to have less market exposure.

◆ Equity hedge strategists look for the companies that have a competitive advantage that will enable them to capitalize on an important economic trend and take long core positions in those companies.

◆ Although the portion of an equity hedge portfolio "within the hedge" may approximate market neutrality, at any given time managers can lose money on both their long and short positions. The portion of the portfolio that is not hedged is, of course, susceptible to all the various caprices of the market.

KEY TERMS

Hedging. The taking of positions to offset changes in economic conditions falling outside the core investment idea, such as purchasing a long position and a short position in a similar stock to offset the effect any changes in the overall level of the equity market will have on the long position.

Leverage. The practice of borrowing to add to an investment position when one believes that the return from the stock position will exceed the cost of the borrowed funds.

Net market exposure. The percentage of the portfolio exposed to market fluctuations because long positions are not matched by equal dollar amounts of short positions. In general terms,

$$\text{Market exposure} = \frac{\text{Long exposure} - \text{Short exposure}}{\text{Capital}}$$

Short selling. Borrowing a stock on collateral and immediately selling it on the market with the intention of buying it back later at a lower price.

Trading positions. Opportunistic positions designed to take advantage of short-term market mispricings and inefficiencies rather than hedge against market decline.

Within the hedge. Phrase used to describe that portion of an equity hedge portfolio in which long positions are matched by equal amounts of short positions.

13

CHAPTER

Emerging
MARKETS

MERGING MARKETS specialists make primarily long investments in the securities of companies in countries with developing or "emerging" financial markets. They use specialized knowledge and an on-the-ground presence in markets in which financial information is often scarce to create an informational advantage that allows them to take advantage of mispricings caused by emerging market inefficiencies. They profit by identifying and investing in undervalued assets.

Emerging markets can be a difficult investment arena because they often present illiquidity, limited market infrastructure, few investment options, likelihood of political turmoil, and barriers to information access. As a result, investors can expose themselves to far greater risks than when they invest in more developed markets. However, the same factors that create risks can also produce very attractive investment opportunities. Because they are primarily long-only, emerging markets strategies are widely shared by mutual fund managers and hedge fund managers.

CORE STRATEGY

THERE ARE DIFFERENT types of emerging markets, but all of them share certain investment features. The majority of these features are the direct result of **MARKET INEFFICIENCIES.** Market inefficiencies result when information on companies is unavailable, hard to come by, or wrong, and therefore assets often remain undervalued. Emerging markets specialists who can mine these markets for undervalued assets and purchase them before the market corrects itself may be rewarded with large investment returns.

Emerging markets are distinguished from both traditional agricultural economies and highly developed economies. They are not simply making the historical transition from an agricultural to an industrialized economy. Rather, most emerging markets are developed to some extent, but their economy is being restructured on the free market model. The emerging market that was "created" in Russia in the 1990s is a perfect example. Many of these countries are learning to function by using the market model rather than some form of bureaucratic control. These markets are changing rapidly at both the macroeconomic level and the company level. They are not entirely trusted by free market investors and are usually trying to change investor sentiment through political and economic reforms. However, the reforms may not be uniformly applied or accepted.

Most emerging markets do not have sophisticated **SECU-RITIES MARKET INFRASTRUCTURE**. Securities market infrastructure includes accounting standards, the availability of trading and financial information, and sophistication of available financial instruments. Ideally, investors can obtain information about company decisions and actions and the results that it has produced. Because this information is not easily available in emerging markets, specialists who are willing to generate their own research can find assets that the market has undervalued due to misperceived or limited information.

The dynamics of emerging markets can be hard to understand. Because these markets are highly volatile, participants often misjudge what they perceive to be economic decline and corruption. For example, Asia has experienced a major shock to its economies and markets in the past year. Some investors ignored Asia's problems for the past five years, and some will ignore its rebound potential after the crash. The Asian markets will probably be slow to recover on a macroeconomic level, but that trend should present excellent investment opportunities for diligent, value-oriented money managers who are not scared off by the macro trends. One approach that emerging markets specialists use to take advantage of such situations is to invest early in markets undergoing political and economic transformations. Often, the assets they select have excellent return potential, not only because they are strong companies, but also because the available information has been distorted by former political systems, a lack of technology, or underdeveloped capital market structures.

Emerging markets specialists usually concentrate on analyzing company fundamentals to identify investments that will allow them to extract the most value from inefficient emerging markets. They anticipate taking advantage of the lack of information flow that keeps all but a few enterprises out of the spotlight and many of them trading at a fraction of their intrinsic value. They must develop a mechanism for uncovering information, because by the time ideas become available to the broader marketplace, much of the potential for returns is gone. To uncover ideas, they not only read newspapers, periodicals, trade journals, and on-line sources but also travel through the countries to meet with local managers and government administrators and keep in constant communication with a network of brokers and contacts in the various markets to discuss political, economic, and market events and specific investment opportunities. The most important component of emerging market research is an on-the-ground presence in the market, especially on-site visits before committing capital.

Emerging market fund managers can invest globally, regionally (e.g., in Latin America), or in a single country (e.g., Russia). Other participants include those who allocate capital on a global basis, shifting their focus based on the changing attractiveness of different markets. Some of them treat emerging markets as one potential asset class along with developed markets and fixed-income investments. They allocate capital to emerging markets when they believe that this asset class offers attractive potential returns compared with investment opportunities in other asset classes. Similarly, regional managers allocate among countries within their region where they perceive the greatest opportunities to invest, while single country managers invest in the best choices within a single country.

INVESTMENT PROCESS

EMERGING MARKETS SPECIALISTS try to capitalize on their ability to gather information in markets in which information does not yet flow as freely as in developed markets. To take advantage of this inefficiency, they engage in fundamental bottom-up research to identify undervalued stocks.

First, they develop early relationships with local brokers, industry participants, and government officials; identify recent or soon-to-be privatized companies; and look at financial reports of companies to understand the variability of their returns and their use of capital. Then they look at the business of the company and assess customers, competitors, and industry trends to determine what to expect in the future. Next, they try to quantify these various issues to determine whether the company is really creating value or simply growing by issuing equity and debt. Finally, after determining growth prospects, the appropriate rates to discount possible risks, and expected currency rates, they only invest if the stock appears to be undervalued to ensure a good margin of safety.

Emerging markets specialists use rigorous fundamental analysis to estimate the value of financial assets as they believe the market will reflect that estimated asset value in the long run. Thus, they make investments when they believe the market has misvalued a security and sell or reassess when the investment approaches their valuation targets. On the downside, they usually sell if a stock declines more than a set stop-loss amount, declines for unexpected reasons, or a material factor changes their valuation. Emerging markets specialists buy stocks when one or several of the following criteria are met: they are undervalued on earnings and/or net asset basis, they have projected high growth in earnings and sales, they are dominant in a product or industry, management is progressive toward shareholder rights, they have good prospects for increased liquidity, or their financials are improving toward international accounting standards. They sell stocks when they are overvalued relative to their industry, market, or other companies in the fund; the market poses an unacceptable risk; or the fundamentals of the market, industry, or company deteriorate. They will give emerging market positions more latitude than they would give a position in a developed market because emerging markets are prone to erratic behavior. Overall, emerging markets specialists try to grow the number of attractive positions in their portfolios while opportunistically paring out those that have become fully valued.

Emerging markets specialists may have biases toward particular industries. They look for businesses that they understand and management teams that are honest, dedicated to their work, and oriented toward a free market model. They seek diversity and invest across sectors they find promising and undervalued.

Many emerging markets do not have the financial infrastructure in place to allow money managers to short sell and hedge, but those that do charge high premiums. Some managers also hedge by shorting American Depositary Receipts (ADRs). An ADR is a U.S. exchange traded security representing ownership in a foreign company. Hedging can help eliminate short-term volatility but may reduce the performance of a portfolio in the long run. In addition, factors other than fundamental value may temporarily move prices in emerging markets. Consequently, to short sell and hedge effectively emerging markets specialists must take into account liquidity flows, unexpected political developments, and changes in emerging market risk premiums. Presently, the costs may outweigh the benefits of short selling and hedging in emerging markets, but as these financial markets become more sophisticated and transaction costs drop, short selling and hedging will become more prevalent.

Money managers only use leverage, when it is available, when they think that they can segment the risk of a particular investment and leverage the attractive risk. The misassessment of risk in the use of leverage can be disastrous, as was witnessed in erosion of hedge funds with leveraged investments in Russia during the collapse of its markets in the summer of 1998. Generally speaking, most emerging markets specialists do not use leverage because it would magnify the already highly volatile nature of these markets.

RISK CONTROL

EMERGING MARKETS ARE often thought of as inherently volatile and risky. An event can create correlations between asset positions that usually would not exist in more developed markets. Stock prices in emerging markets can become depressed for reasons other than the underlying company losing real value. Emerging markets specialists attempt to control these risks by diversifying the exposure in their portfolio across companies, industries, or markets; attempting to purchase assets at low valuation levels to provide a margin for error; segmenting risk by building a portfolio with different kinds of risk; and hedging long exposures where possible and appropriate. They try to buy assets with prices that will not all move together in response to market forces, and they are careful to make sure that long and short positions do not represent the same investment idea. Why? Because this uniformity would magnify risk rather than reduce it. Not only can a portfolio with diverse positions reap the rewards of long-term return potential, it can also withstand unexpected short-term pricing risks or risks peculiar to an individual market. To restrict maximum exposure to any one country or company, some emerging markets specialists use macroeconomic weighting models to restrict maximum exposure to any one country or company. In general, they keep enough positions in their fund to get the benefits of diversification, but few enough so that each position is meaningful to the fund's return. Although traditional investors manage risk by looking at volatility and how assets have correlated historically, that approach will often ignore new relationships developing between different assets. Consequently, in addition to traditional measures, some emerging markets specialists use their own forecasts and intuition to estimate future volatility and correlation between assets.

The inherent volatility in emerging markets is the price of having exposure to undervalued, high-growth investment opportunities. Because the emerging market strategy is generally a long-run strategy, emerging markets specialists see the numerous steep declines that punctuate the general long-term ascent of these economies as great opportunities to buy cheap assets. In the long term, an emerging market usually becomes less volatile as it develops a larger private sector and domestic capital becomes a larger portion of market capitalization.

ADVANTAGES/DISADVANTAGES

EMERGING MARKETS CAN be difficult investments because of the paucity of information, poor accounting, lack of proper legal systems, unsophisticated local investors, political and economic turmoil, and companies with dishonest and unqualified managers. As a result of these problems, nonspecialists expose themselves to far greater risks when they invest in emerging markets than when they invest in more developed markets. However, emerging markets specialists find these markets appealing because of the profit possibilities that these same difficulties create. What some would call difficulties, emerging markets specialists call opportunities. A market that is volatile and unpredictable in the short run because information about companies is hard to come by and distortions run rampant is also a market full of mispricings; this creates significant openings for investors willing to do the extra work to uncover hidden situations. The structural changes in these markets create inefficiencies that are eventually driven out, yielding outstanding returns to those who invest in the early stages.

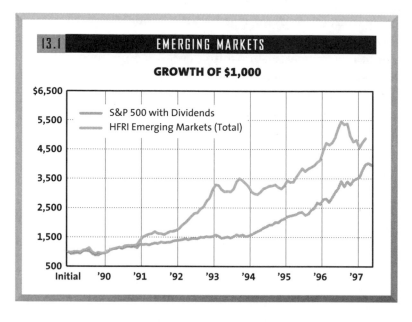

13.1 EMERGING MARKETS

GROWTH OF $1,000

Legend:
— S&P 500 with Dividends
— HFRI Emerging Markets (Total)

Y-axis: $6,500 / 5,500 / 4,500 / 3,500 / 2,500 / 1,500 / 500

X-axis: Initial '90 '91 '92 '93 '94 '95 '96 '97

PERFORMANCE

FROM JANUARY 1990 to March 1998, they recorded average annualized returns of 21.22, with an annualized standard deviation of 13.48. These returns were nearly 3 percent higher than the Standard and Poor's 500 index of blue-chip stocks for the same period, at a slightly higher level of volatility. In 1991 and 1993, emerging markets funds showed their potential for enormous returns, registering returns of 45.40 and 79.22 percent. However, they returned only 3.38 in 1994 and 0.69 in 1995 and showed a loss of 3.35 in 1990. These figures underscore the point that high returns in emerging markets in the long run come at a cost of short-term volatility *(see Appendix C for updated performance)*.

SUMMARY POINTS

PROFIT OPPORTUNITY

◆ Emerging markets specialists use specialized knowledge and an on-the-ground presence in markets in which financial information is often scarce to create an informational advantage that allows them to take advantage of mispricings caused by emerging market inefficiencies.

◆ Most emerging markets are developed to some extent, but their economy is being restructured on the free market model.

◆ Because these markets are highly volatile, the participants often misjudge what they perceive to be economic decline and corruption.

◆ Markets that are volatile and unpredictable in the short run because information about companies is hard to come by and often distorted are also markets full of mispricings that provide investment opportunities.

SOURCE OF RETURN

◆ Because emerging markets do not have sophisticated securities market infrastructure, specialists who are willing to generate their own information by doing their own research in the country can find assets that the market has undervalued because it does not have or has misperceived this information.

◆ Emerging markets specialists can capture superior returns in the long run by venturing carefully into areas of the market in which information can be obtained but is not readily available. They must develop a mechanism for uncovering information, because by the time ideas become available in the marketplace, much of the potential for returns is gone.

◆ The inherent volatility in emerging markets is the price of having exposure to undervalued, high-growth investment opportunities.

◆ The structural changes in these markets create inefficiencies that are eventually driven out, yielding outstanding returns to those who invested in the early stages.

INVESTMENT PROCESS

◆ Emerging markets specialists concentrate on analyzing company fundamentals to extract the most value from inefficient emerging markets.

◆ The most important component of emerging market research is an on-the-ground presence in the market.

◆ Often, the costs outweigh the benefits of short selling and hedging in emerging markets, but as these financial markets get more sophisticated and transaction costs drop, short selling and hedging will become more prevalent in emerging markets.

KEY TERMS

Emerging market. A market that is changing rapidly at the macroeconomic and company level, usually because it is restructuring on the free market model.

Global investors. Investors who consider emerging markets to be one potential asset class, along with developed markets and fixed-income securities, and allocate capital to emerging markets when they believe that they offer attractive potential returns compared with other asset classes.

Market inefficiencies. Pricing disparities caused by a lack of information about a market or company or by a distortion of the information that is available.

Securities market infrastructure. The means of making investments and tracking financial information, including accounting standards, availability of trading and financial information, and sophistication of available financial instruments.

CHAPTER

14

Short
SELLING

HORT SELLERS SEEK to profit from a decline in the value of stocks. The strategy involves selling a security that the seller does not own to take advantage of an anticipated price decline. The short seller borrows the securities from a third party to deliver them to the purchaser. The short seller eventually repurchases the securities on the open market to return them to the third-party lender. If the short seller can repurchase the stock at a lower price than what he or she sold it for, then he or she makes a profit. In addition, the short seller earns interest on the cash proceeds from the short sale of stock. However, if the price of the stock rises, then he or she incurs a loss. Generally, a short seller must pledge other securities or cash equal to the market price of the borrowed securities with the lender.

MANY HEDGE FUND STRATEGIES short sell as a component of strategy, usually as a hedging device or as a trading technique used to take advantage of short-term pricing inefficiencies. However, certain managers will construct short-only portfolios to take advantage of the fact that short selling can provide both fixed income and trading profits. In practice, short selling has fared poorly for most of the 1990s bull market because even mediocre and overpriced stocks have been carried upward by the general momentum of the market. Good opportunities to sell short simply have not been plentiful. As a result, short-only managers have become a rare breed, but more are sure to resurface in the next bear market. In the light of that eventuality, this chapter will explain short selling as a distinct investment strategy rather than as a hedging or trading technique.

CORE STRATEGY

SHORT SELLING SPECIALISTS borrow stock owned by a long investor and sell it on the market with the intention of buying it back later at a lower price after the market corrects itself. By selling the stock short, the short seller creates a restricted cash asset (the proceeds from the sale) and a liability (he or she must return the borrowed shares at some future date). Technically, a short sale does not require an investment, but it does require collateral, usually cash or relatively liquid U.S. Treasury securities. The short seller must pay any dividends paid out on the borrowed stock, so it can be costly to sell short stocks with a high yield. However, the proceeds from the short sale are then held as a restricted credit by the brokerage firm that holds the account and the short seller earns interest on it (the short interest rebate). The amount of restricted credit is adjusted daily as the portfolio is marked to the market (revalued at current market prices). As the market value of the shorted stock declines (becomes profitable), the restricted cash (the collateral) is released to become free cash, which earns a higher rate of return. If the value of the shorted stock increases (becomes unprofitable), the short seller must add to the restricted credit, either by selling other investments or by borrowing funds.

INVESTMENT PROCESS

THE BEST WAY to demonstrate a short seller's source of returns is with examples that compare a short sale with a comparable long investment:

The examples contained in Table 14.1 on the following two pages demonstrate that theoretically a short-only portfolio of stocks that pay small or no dividends can outperform a long portfolio in certain market environments because of the added income from the interest on the collateral and the short rebate. Despite this advantage, short selling as a stand-alone strategy became very rare in the 1990s.

ADVANTAGES/DISADVANTAGES

THE BULL MARKET of the 1990s had nearly driven short selling as a stand-alone investment strategy into extinction. Besides the fact that it is hard to find overvalued stocks to profitably sell short when the whole market is charging, short selling can suffer from a number of other disadvantages that relate to market conditions. The potential losses on a long position are finite, whereas the potential losses on a short sale are infinite. However, the potential gain on a short sale is limited. If an investor buys a stock at 50, the price of that stock can only decline to 0, a maximum of 100 percent gain. On the downside, that stock can increase in value infinitely. So if it appreciates to 150, the short seller can lose 200 percent. Because gains are limited and losses are theoretically unlimited, short sellers often have their entire net worth at stake.

In the past, many short sellers made profits by shorting "overhyped" stocks that had received attention out of line with the intrinsic value of the company. However, in the 1990s, these overvalued stocks were carried upward by the general momentum of the market. Overvalued stocks do not tend to collapse without a catalytic event, and those had been few and far between in the 1990s. It does not matter if stocks are overvalued if there is nothing to bring this overvaluation to the market's attention. Short sellers also receive little help from Wall Street analysts who are reluctant to issue sell recommendations.

On the upside, short selling strategies provide a yield regardless of capital gains or losses, a high level of liquidity, and can produce high investment returns in bear markets. Short selling as an investment strategy proved unsustainable for all but a few investment managers in the 1990s bull market. This is not surprising considering we were in the midst of the longest period in history without a major market correction. However, as the bear market returns, then short selling will reappear as a viable investment strategy.

14.1   INVESTMENT PROCESS SCENARIOS 1–4

SCENARIO 1

A LONG INVESTOR with $100,000 in capital to invest purchases 20,000 shares of stock A, a non-dividend-paying common stock, at $5 per share, and over the course of one year the price of the stock increases by $1, to $6 per share.

Beginning investment (20,000 shares of stock A @ $5)	$100,000
Ending investment (20,000 shares of stock A @ $6)	$120,000
Gain	$20,000
As a percentage of investment	20%

SCENARIO 2

A SHORT SELLER with $100,000 in 1-year U.S. Treasury securities with a 6 percent yield uses this capital as collateral to borrow 20,000 shares of stock B at $5 per share, and over the course of one year the price of the stock declines $1, to $4 per share.

Beginning positions:

Long: Collateral of $100,000 of 1-year 6% U.S. Treasury securities
Short: 20,000 shares of stock B at $5 per share
Returns:

Gain on short sale of stock B	$20,000
Interest on U.S. Treasury securities at 6%	$6,000
Interest rebate on proceeds from short sale of stock B assuming an interest rate of 5%	$4,490
Earnings on cash freed by short gain	$614
Total gain	$31,104
As a percentage of equity	31.1%

PERFORMANCE

FROM JANUARY 1990 to March 1998, short selling registered average annualized returns of 1.01 percent, with an annualized standard deviation of 18.43. As would be expected, they registered substantial returns in the retractions of 1990 and 1994 (36.21 and 18.54 percent) and a modest 10 percent return in 1992. They registered sig-

SCENARIO 3

A LONG INVESTOR with $100,000 in capital to invest purchases 20,000 shares of stock A, a non-dividend-paying common stock, at $5 per share, and over the course of one year the price of the stock decreases by $1, to $4 per share.

Beginning investment (20,000 shares of stock A @ $5)	$100,000
Ending investment (20,000 shares of stock A @ $4)	$80,000
Loss	($20,000)
As a percentage of investment	20%

SCENARIO 4

A SHORT SELLER with $100,000 in 1-year U.S. Treasury securities with a 6 percent yield uses this capital as collateral to borrow 20,000 shares of stock B at $5 per share, and over the course of one year the price of the stock appreciates $1, to $6 per share.

Beginning positions:

Long: Collateral of $100,000 of 1-year 6% U.S. Treasury securities

Short: 20,000 shares of stock B at $5 per share

Returns:

Loss on short sale of stock B	($20,000)
Interest on U.S. Treasury securities at 6%	$6,000
Interest rebate on proceeds from short sale of stock B assuming an interest rate of 5%	$5,510
Margin interest paid on short loss	($824)
Total loss	($9,314)
As a percentage of equity	9.3%

nificant losses in 1991, 1993, and 1994 to 1995. The swings from positive to negative returns raised the general level of volatility for the strategy. The short seller fund's correlation statistic of .4603 reveals a high degree of sensitivity to general changes in stock prices (their Beta statistic of -1.02, which measures the magnitude of correlation, shows that their returns move inversely to the prices of stocks.) *(See Appendix C for updated performance.)*

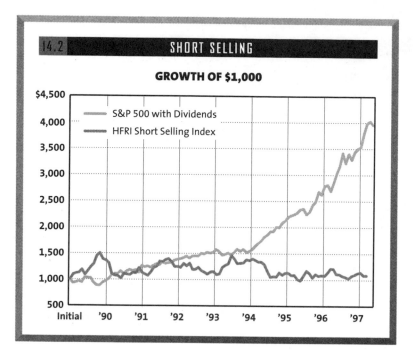

14.2   SHORT SELLING

GROWTH OF $1,000

- S&P 500 with Dividends
- HFRI Short Selling Index

SUMMARY POINTS

PROFIT OPPORTUNITY

◆ Certain managers will construct short-only portfolios to take advantage of the fact that, theoretically, short selling can out-perform a long strategy because it provides both fixed income and trading profits.

◆ On the upside, short selling strategies provide a yield regardless of capital gains or losses, a very high level of liquidity, and can produce high investment returns in bear markets.

◆ The 1990s have witnessed the longest period in history without a major market correction. Short sellers have fared poorly during this period.

SOURCE OF RETURN

◆ Short selling specialists borrow overvalued stock owned by a long investor and sell it on the market with the intention of buying it back later at a lower price after the market corrects itself.

◆ Theoretically, a short-only portfolio of stocks that pay small or no dividends will outperform a long portfolio because of the added income from the interest on the collateral and the short rebate.

INVESTMENT PROCESS

◆ It is hard to find overvalued stocks to profitably sell short when the whole market is charging.

◆ Overhyped stocks do not tend to collapse without a catalytic event, and those have been few and far between in the 1990s. It does not matter if stocks are overvalued if there is nothing to bring this overvaluation to the market's attention.

KEY TERMS

Catalytic event. A near-term event that will change the market's perception of a particular stock.

Collateral. Cash or very liquid securities that are held as a deposit on borrowed stock.

Mark to market. To determine the price one can get today for currently owned securities.

Short interest rebate. The interest earned on the cash proceeds from a short sale of stock.

MAKING AN
Investment

PART

II

CHAPTER

15

Investing In
HEDGE
FUNDS

IKE MOST INVESTMENT DECISIONS, investing in hedge funds is a rational process that begins with an investment goal and results in making one or more investment selections. The process enables the selection of investments with a reasonable expectation of achieving the investment objectives. The goal of hedge fund investors is to achieve certain results by allocating assets to one or a combination of hedge funds that gives access to alternative investment strategies. It is important to follow a methodology in constructing a portfolio of hedge funds: to create a framework within which to select investments and to evaluate and monitor the portfolio's risk and performance. Such a framework provides an efficient information feedback loop that allows the adjustment, refinement, and successful management of a multiple fund or manager investment portfolio.

To properly analyze hedge fund strategies, combine

them to construct portfolios, and monitor such investments, an investor must have access to the underlying investment portfolio. Without this information only a one-sided evaluation can be conducted, ignoring the actual risk exposures of the strategy. The collapse of a number of secretive hedge funds in 1998 revealed the excessive risk that some managers will take with investment assets when a veil of secrecy protects them from accountability to investors. Those failures underscore the fact that prudent investing requires investment portfolio transparency and the evaluation of risk exposure. Blind investments should be avoided.

The following is a suggested framework for selecting hedge funds and alternative investment strategies and combining them in a portfolio. Although it is intended for investors who want to construct a multiple-manager portfolio, the concepts can be applied to the selection of a single manager or hedge fund as well. There are three basic steps in making an allocation to hedge funds:

1 **Planning the investment.** This is the stage in which investors decide what they wish to achieve and how they will achieve those goals. It includes a) defining the investment objective(s) and b) establishing investment parameters for individual hedge funds, for strategies, and for the portfolio as a whole.

2 **Choosing a structure and the appropriate strategies.** The second step is to research and then select the investment structure(s) that will be used in the program to access hedge fund strategies that best satisfy the investment goals. To determine the appropriate structure(s) and strategies, investors must apply the objectives and parameters established in the planning stage to the available structure and strategy options. The two components are a) selection of the optimal structure(s) and b) selection of suitable strategies.

3 **Selecting hedge funds or managers.** The third step is the manager search, in which individual hedge funds and/or investment managers that satisfy the structure, strategy, and other parameter requirements established in steps 1 and 2 are evaluated for investment. The individual hedge funds or hedge fund managers are researched, and the funds that best fit the parameters and fulfill the objectives are selected for the portfolio.

STEP ONE

PLANNING THE INVESTMENT

ALTHOUGH ALTERNATIVE investment strategies are dissimilar in many ways to more traditional investments, the fundamentals of prudent investing are not. Decisions to invest in these strategies must be based on realistic goals and expectations. To establish realistic goals, investors must have an understanding of the available products and services. The first fourteen chapters of this book present an overview of a variety of investment approaches and methods of investing that will help investors understand the hedge fund industry and formulate realistic goals.

As discussed, a hedge fund can be housed in any of a number of investment structures. Managers use one or more of a variety of alternative investment strategies that provide a diverse range of investment exposures and risk/reward characteristics. Although these strategies are diverse and involve more complex approaches than traditional investments, they are all understandable and definable. The investment process therefore involves considering what the best hedge fund structure(s) for the investment will be and the risks and benefits of accessing the different strategies through that structure.

The planning process is the critical first step in making a hedge fund investment. The investor must form a framework for structuring and managing a multiple-manager hedge fund investment program. The first step is to clearly define what they expect to achieve by investing in hedge funds; then the investor can establish investment parameters which guide how those objectives are to be met.

DEFINING PORTFOLIO OBJECTIVES

THE FIRST STEP that an investor should take is to define the objectives of the portfolio. The objectives make explicit what the investor expects to achieve from the hedge fund investment. These usually include return and risk measures such as level, consistency, volatility, maximum loss, and correlation to stocks or bonds. Other objectives might address leverage (both borrowing and derived), liquidity of the investment, and region and country exposures. Important structural issues pertaining to custody of the assets and fund transparency may also be stated as an objective. Although almost all investors share achieving investment returns, either absolute or relative to some benchmark, as a main objective, individual investors may have one or more objectives of differing priorities, ranging from pursuing risk-adjusted return to accessing spe-

15.1 A HYPOTHETICAL SET OF PORTFOLIO OBJECTIVES

Return per Annum	15%
Leverage	Nonborrowing
Volatility	Less than 5%
Maximum Loss	Less than 10%
Correlation	Less than 0.30
Transparency	Daily

cific types of financial instruments or investment strategies. Table 15.1 above illustrates an example of a possible set of portfolio objectives.

Investors may modify portfolio objectives throughout the planning process, particularly if they are learning about the industry and the various opportunities that it presents.

ESTABLISHING INVESTMENT PARAMETERS

WHILE PORTFOLIO OBJECTIVES make explicit what investors wish to achieve through a hedge fund investment, investment parameters help to control how those portfolio objectives are accomplished. They include the rules and guidelines that determine how an investment portfolio is constructed and operated. Parameters are the constraints, requirements, inclusions, and exclusions imposed on the investor's selection of hedge fund structures and strategies and the operation of the investment program. These can be self-imposed by investors or required by regulatory bodies.

Investment parameters can be applied on three levels:
1 to the overall portfolio;
2 to each strategy;
3 to each individual manager or fund.

Figure 15.2, right, represents the investment parameter hierarchy.

Working up from the bottom of the pyramid, the invest-

15.2   INVESTMENT PARAMETERS HIERARCHY

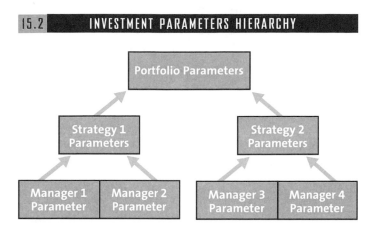

ment parameters imposed on the selection of managers for a particular strategy in combination are designed to achieve the overall strategy parameters. Similarly, the parameters established for the strategies in combination allow for the portfolio parameters to be met.

Investment parameters may also refine or elaborate portfolio objectives. For example, a portfolio objective of using exchange-listed equities only will have an investment parameter that limits the hedge funds that will be considered to those investing in such securities. Thus, investors should consider five useful categories when establishing investment parameters:

1 **Regulatory restrictions.** Constraints placed on investment activities by governmental agencies regulating securities, commodities, taxation, banking, insurance, and retirement assets must be incorporated into the investment parameters, according to the type of investors involved.

2 **Investment policy limitations.** Self-imposed restrictions are based on the investor's interpretation of investment guidelines or on prudent investment standards.

3 **Risk control considerations.** Specific constraints for risk-related issues and market exposures include the use of leverage, volatility of returns, and correlation of returns to other investments in the portfolio.

4 Performance controls. Appropriate target ranges are set for returns, volatility, and other performance measures.

5 Portfolio composition methodology. Guidelines are constructed for allocating assets, diversifying holdings, and balancing the portfolio on an ongoing basis.

Investment parameters may be established for individual fund managers based on the types of instruments in which they invest and trade, the length of their track record, the amount of assets they have under management, their greatest losing period or maximum drawdown, the liquidity of the fund, the minimum investment required, historic risk measures, and actual risk probabilities. Certain trading strategies or financial instruments might be required to be included in or excluded from the portfolio (e.g., equity strategies only, but no illiquid securities). Portfolio-level parameters could also require that the funds be invested only in U.S. securities or in specific industry sectors or, alternatively, that the portfolio be globally diversified. Considerations include instruments and markets, investment methods, leverage, asset size, liquidity, and performance (absolute or relative, target and floor).

"Stress testing" the portfolio is a valuable analytical tool; basically, it is an evaluation of the portfolio's performance under a series of "what if" scenarios. These scenarios address the objectives and parameters set in the planning stage. If noncorrelation to stock and bond markets is an objective, each manager and the combination of managers must be evaluated. What if the stock market drops 30 percent? What if interest rates are increased by 50 basis points? To perform a completely accurate stress test requires knowledge of the investments in each manager's portfolio so that overall market exposures can be accurately determined. Assumptions about how the instruments will behave under the various scenarios may be based on historic or other methods of estimation. By considering the impact of various market scenarios, investors can develop performance expectations for each hedge fund in the portfolio under different conditions, anticipate the expected correlation of the returns from the different funds, and therefore better forecast the overall performance of the portfolio. In the final portfolio, this forecast should correspond to the original objectives.

PLANNING TIPS

THE INVESTMENT PARAMETERS for individual fund managers may differ considerably from those of the portfolio as a whole. For example, the volatility of returns allowable for any particular hedge fund in the portfolio might be greater than the return volatility objectives of the total portfolio because of the offsetting nature of the volatility of noncorrelated strategies *(see Table 15.2)*. By diversifying the portfolio across these various funds, the portfolio manager reduces the return volatility of the portfolio as a whole.

MINIMIZING AND NEUTRALIZING RISK

RISK AT THE MANAGER, strategy, and portfolio levels should be addressed in the investment parameters. One of the main reasons for establishing investment parameters is to manage or avoid existing and potential investment risks. Investment risk can take many forms, including:

◆ the general condition of markets in which one trades
◆ creditworthiness
◆ exposure to potential fraud
◆ manager incompetence
◆ misrepresentation of investment activities
◆ form of investment vehicle
◆ government regulations
◆ the underlying instruments used by the fund
◆ industry concentration
◆ the investment strategy selected.

Obviously, certain risks are specific to certain positions and funds, and others apply to the portfolio as a whole. How the risks of any particular fund relate to the risk associated with the portfolio as a whole must be evaluated, and the two sets of risk must be balanced relative to the benefits provided. At that point the investor should decide whether to avoid, neutralize, minimize, or accept each risk. Risks can be avoided or minimized by:

◆ not investing in a strategy or with a particular manager.
◆ selecting a manager who has addressed the particular risk through the investment approach (for example, by hedging foreign exchange risk).
◆ establishing investment guidelines that contain the risks (for example, limiting the exposure to any single issuer).
◆ combining strategies that are complementary (such as, when a market condition that is risky for one approach is favorable for the other).
◆ incorporating a risk-monitoring program.

If an investor allocates assets to a strategy or a manager with full knowledge of the risk but without taking any precautions for it, then the risk becomes an accepted part of the investment. An investor who invests in a non-transparent fund has accepted the risk that anything could happen.

Often full attention is devoted to obvious risks and too little attention to less likely ones. Proper probabilities are assigned to risk scenarios that are highly likely but probabilities of zero are assigned to those risk scenarios with lower, but not zero, probabilities of occurring. All investment strategies have flaws that can produce substantial losses of capital, and, as remote as any risk may seem, it should be recognized and addressed accordingly.

DIVERSIFICATION

BY DIVERSIFYING PORTFOLIOS across strategies and financial instruments, the overall portfolio risk is reduced by limiting the effect that any one exposure can have on the portfolio as a whole. A primary goal of fund diversification is to include funds in the portfolio that will perform well in different market environments. This is accomplished by combining a variety of strategies. Funds that use the same strategies will often perform similarly to one another. For example, a portfolio of ten fixed-income arbitrage hedge funds will not reduce risk significantly when each allocation represents a similar investment idea. A portfolio with few limiting parameters allows for broad diversification across strategies and instruments. Keep in mind that parameters that attempt to screen out risk may also narrow the universe of acceptable strategies or hedge funds. With fewer acceptable funds to choose from, the final portfolio may be less diversified. In this case, the investor has effectively traded one kind of risk for another. If the investment parameters limit the scope of the portfolio, diversification should be focused on the eligible approaches and number of acceptable strategies.

NUMBER OF FUNDS

THE OPTIMAL NUMBER of hedge funds to include in a portfolio is the subject of some debate. Expert opinions recommend from five to fifty. Of course, the number of funds included is often determined by the amount of investment capital and the desired form of investment. Because larger and more established hedge funds have higher minimum investment requirements, fewer of these funds can be included in a portfolio compared with funds that require lower minimum investments. If separate accounts are used, the minimum investment amount per manager will usually be significantly larger than those required for investing in comingled funds.

STEP TWO

STRUCTURE AND STRATEGY SELECTION

THE SELECTION PROCESS applies the investment parameters to the construction of the portfolio. It begins with the identification of acceptable investment structures. Once an appropriate structure is chosen, the next step is to select strategies.

SELECTING STRUCTURES

CHOOSE AN INVESTMENT structure based on its ability to satisfy the investment parameters and objectives. Hedge fund structures and investment vehicles are covered in detail in Chapter 2, but some critical points are worth reviewing here.

A threshold question is whether the investment will be made in existing fund structures or in separately managed accounts. If control and custody over the assets to be invested are required, the investment must be made through a separate account, as investing in a fund gives up custody and all control over the investment activities. If custody and control are not an issue, then an existing fund structure should work. Another issue in selecting an investment structure is transparency. Transparency refers to investors' ability to "see through" a manager's portfolio to the underlying investments (transparency is covered in more detail in Chapter 16). Some managers only allow transparency in a separately managed account. Others allow it in their funds as well. If transparency is an issue but custody and control are not, then investing in transparent funds is also an appropriate solution.

SELECTING STRATEGIES

A LARGE PORTION of this book (Chapters 3 to14) is devoted to a discussion of the various hedge fund strategies. They represent a broad range of risk and return characteristics. Even within strategy classifications, there is distinct variation. Strategies should be based on a reasonable expectation that they will:

1 achieve performance objectives
2 satisfy parameter requirements
3 operate under the selected hedge fund structure.

MANAGER/FUND SEARCH AND SELECTION

MANAGER SEARCH PROCEDURE

ALTHOUGH THE LARGE number and diversity of hedge funds that must be analyzed may seem to be a daunting task, identifying the structure and strategies that are acceptable focuses the choice of possible funds and managers. Parameters—such as amount of assets under management, experience of the fund manager, and instruments traded—reduce the field of candidates further, resulting in a short list that can be analyzed more thoroughly. A closer inspection of the managers—even those who describe their strategies similarly—will reveal variations and nuances in style and specialization. Managers who practice similar strategies do not necessarily have the same talent for doing so. However, comparing managers' performance numbers can be problematic because a particular manager's performance numbers may, on closer inspection, be revealed to be an amalgam of inconsistent investment approaches implemented over time. Investment managers' promotional materials and disclosure documents can be helpful, but in many cases these are written in such broad terms that their usefulness is limited. The need for transparency for prudent investing begins at this stage. The analysis of a manager's investment portfolio is the only way to understand its investment activities and the associated benefits and risks.

Once a list of the manager's funds is selected, a more detailed evaluation is conducted. The purpose of hedge fund evaluation is to develop a sense of what kind of future performance can reasonably be expected. Funds are selected for the portfolio based on how each fund is expected to perform on an absolute basis and how each is expected to perform in relation to the other hedge funds in the portfolio. Performance expectations are both general and specific and should correspond to the level of ongoing monitoring and evaluation that investors intend to conduct.

The evaluation process involves the collection and evaluation of all available material, past and present, to arrive at a set of future expectations for the fund. Quantitative and qualitative investment criteria used for this purpose are described below. They are also used as the basis for ongoing portfolio monitoring and performance evaluation (ongoing risk and performance monitoring is covered in Chapter 16). These criteria help the investor and the portfolio manager develop a set of reasonable expectations about future performance of the funds on which to construct the portfolio.

◆ **Quantitative analysis.** Quantitative analysis is the statistical evaluation of the past performance and investment activity of hedge funds and separate accounts. This process involves gathering and analyzing such data using various measures of risk, reward, and risk/reward relationships. Analysis of risk and performance statistics also allows investors to compare one investment with another or with peer groups and benchmarks.

By itself, quantitative analysis of the performance data is a perfect evaluation of the past results but an unreliable predictor of future performance. As long as all conditions were the same during the period of evaluation and will continue to stay exactly the same in the future, a statistical study of the past is very helpful in predicting the future. However, conditions change, and past performance, although an important input, can by itself be highly misleading and is just one of number of factors that help indicate expected future performance.

In addition, because many hedge funds have been established only recently, the performance data for these managers often only reflect a particular economic climate. During the 1990s, new funds have benefited from very favorable market conditions. Although most of the managers of these funds are practitioners of investment strategies designed to profit in a variety of market conditions, many of them have only recently experienced a true bear market. Relying entirely on statistical analysis often results in poor investment decisions, but it is a common practice because it is the easiest analysis to perform.

◆ **Qualitative analysis.** Qualitative analysis looks behind the performance numbers at how they were achieved, who the firm's principle individuals are, and what the make up of their business is. Qualitative analysis is critical in evaluating a fund manager's historic performance. If a fund manager's past performance is to be of any use in predicting future performance, then there must be continuity. Thorough qualitative evaluations take into account past and current market conditions, the latent risks and benefits of the strategy, the consistency of the fund manager's investment operation over time, and the strengths and weaknesses of the individuals making investment decisions.

The investor should look first for continuity in the fund manager's approach and application of a chosen strategy and, second, in the nature of the markets to which the manager applied the strategy. For example, the track record of a fund manager that reflects specialized arbitrage trades will not be useful for forecasting future performance if the market in question becomes more efficient, wiping out arbitrage opportunities or becomes more volatile, creating excessive risk for leveraged strategies.

Similarly, the track record of a systematic manager would provide little insight into future performance if the manager changed disciplines and began investing on a discretionary basis. In addition, a fund manager's past performance does not indicate how the manager will cope with a different market environment or whether the manager's strategy can generate similar returns with an increase or decrease in assets under management.

◆ **Summary.** Because an investment in a hedge fund is an investment in an entrepreneurial business operation, investors should seek to answer the question: What business is the manager really in? The various areas of the business that should be reviewed include operations, personnel backgrounds, investment methodology, and performance record.

BUSINESS OPERATIONS

IN REVIEWING THE OPERATION of the business, assess the various aspects of the business's internal functions, including management, trading, research, operations, compliance, and client service. Outside professionals—such as the firm's accountant, auditor, attorney, prime broker, bank, administrator, and custodian—should be evaluated as well. In addition, the information systems on which a firm relies—including trading, back office, and research systems—should be considered. Also address contingency plans for backing up the information systems and the existence of an alternative operating location to maintain continuity of portfolio management in the event of a crisis.

PERSONNEL BACKGROUNDS

BEFORE INVESTING IN a hedge fund, questions that should be answered include the following: What is the regulatory history of key personnel? Have any of them led any "past lives" as investment managers, requiring further investigation? Where is their money invested? What do references and background checks reveal about them? Registrations with the Securities and Exchange Commission, Commodities Futures Trading Commission, National Association of Securities Dealers, and National Futures Association are important information sources. Check with such agencies to learn more about the manager's regulatory history. The answers to these background questions give an investor a clearer idea of who the fund manager is and help indicate what actions can be expected in the future.

INVESTMENT METHODOLOGY

EVEN MANAGERS WHO use similar strategies may implement those strategies in different ways. Therefore, it is important to learn as much as possible about a manager's investment methodology. Many of these considerations are discussed in the Core Strategy and Investment Process sections of the strategy chapters in this book. Each manager should be able to describe all material aspects of their investment activities including: the fund's sources of expected return; use of leverage; liquidity; diversification; position concentrations; portfolio turnover; methods for evaluating securities; research sources; investment universe; use of derivatives and short selling; hedging practices; significant risks; and risk control procedures. Determine the factors that influence decisions to put positions on and take them off and how the actual trading is accomplished as well as whether the fund's investment methodology has changed over time. The most consistent funds usually have well-refined and tested investment methodologies. On top of these basics, investors should find out who makes the fund's investment decisions, and what the contingency plan is to safeguard the portfolio if a key individual becomes incapacitated. In sum, it is important to examine the process that a fund goes through to arrive at its final investment decisions as well as how, mechanically, the investments are made.

PERFORMANCE RECORD

THE FIRST THING that most investors will look at is a fund's performance record. However, prudent investors will not take that record at face value. They will examine how the performance record reflects past and current market conditions. They will note that managers with longer track records tend to be more established and to have dealt with a wider variety of market situations. On the other hand, each year managers with long, stable track records run into difficulties and post significant losses.

Investors should also determine how any strategy changes made by a fund are reflected in its performance record. In addition, investors should look at how a fund's assets under management have changed over time. For example, as assets have grown, how has the manager handled increased size? Does the fund use a niche strategy that cannot efficiently invest the larger asset base? In sum, investors should question a fund's performance record rather than accept it at face value.

The selection of hedge funds/managers is the final step in the structuring process. The number selected and the basis for their inclusion in a diversified portfolio will be based on parameters established at the planning stage. The risk and performance expectations material to each hedge fund manager's selection also form the basis for ongoing monitoring after the investment is made.

SUMMARY

◆ Investments in hedge funds should follow a well defined and structured process that provides an efficient information feedback loop that allows the adjustment, refinement, and successful management of a multiple manager or fund investment portfolio.

◆ Prudent investing requires portfolio transparency to:
   1 Understand the investment merits and risk exposures of the investment strategy
   2 Select managers and funds
   3 Monitor the day-to-day risk exposures.

◆ The steps in making a hedge fund allocation include:
   1 Planning the investment
      a Defining the portfolio objectives
      b Establishing investment parameters
   2 Choosing a structure and selecting strategies that satisfy the objectives and parameters established in the planning stage
   3 Selecting hedge fund managers that
      a Have a reasonable expectation of achieving performance objectives
      b Satisfy parameter requirements
      c Will operate under the selected hedge fund structure.

CHAPTER 16

After the
INITIAL
ALLOCATION

ONGOING DUE DILIGENCE

S DISCUSSED IN Chapter 15, due diligence is an intelligence-gathering process in which all the information available about a fund or manager is collected and analyzed. The purpose is to determine the nature and potential benefits and risks associated with the fund's investment strategy and the structure used to access that strategy and to develop expectations about future investment activities and performance. These conclusions and expectations allow the investor to determine whether the fund is a suitable investment. However, the work does not end when an investment selection is made; due diligence is an ongoing process.

Due diligence produces information about how assets can be expected to be managed in the future. It identifies the risks associated with the managers and strategies. Steps are taken to eliminate, neutralize, or contain those risks. A variety of important factors are identified and representations are made during the due diligence process prior to investment. They form the foundation upon which future investment activity and performance expectations are based. Funds or managers are in turn selected with reliance on these expectations. If the factors change, the basis for the future expectations, and thus the investment selection, no longer exists. Therefore, the ongoing due diligence process involves keeping up with the qualitative aspects of the manager or hedge fund as well as the quantifiable aspects of the investment portfolio. How investors monitor the risk and performance of any particular allocation on an ongoing basis is partly dependent on the degree of portfolio transparency.

QUALITATIVE RISK CONTROL: HISTORIC PROBLEM AREAS

ONGOING QUALITATIVE due diligence involves periodically reviewing the various factors (often, but not always stated as parameters), outside of investment activities and performance, that were material to selecting a manager or fund. If these have changed, the rationale for being in the investment may no longer exist. The following are some of the areas in which problems have occurred with hedge funds. As they are often repeated, it is advisable to consider them on an ongoing basis.

◆ **Assets exceed strategy capacity.** Many of the hedge fund strategies profit from inefficiencies in niches of limited size. However, the high returns often attract more investor money than can be invested in the manner in which the original returns were generated. This may lead to more risky behavior by the manager to maintain return levels, such as an expansion into areas in which the manager has limited experience, or the increased use of leverage or more risky investments.

◆ **Market inefficiency no longer exists.** Certain strategies capitalize on new market inefficiencies. Success attracts new investment capital and more competitors to the area. As more capital flows in, the inefficiency becomes reduced, resulting in lower returns or other changes that increase risk.

◆ **End of the trend.** Many investment strategies are following and dependent on a market environment trend, such as declining interest rates. A slowdown, end, or reversal of the trend will usually adversely affect the strategy's performance.

◆ **Latent problems.** Disguised risks and exposure weaknesses may exist in a portfolio. They include concentrations that are susceptible to changes in market conditions that are not a source of return. For example, a strategy that invests in financially weak companies may have a substantial bankruptcy risk. A slight increase in the number of defaults may result in significant losses for such a strategy.

◆ **Leverage.** Leveraging both magnifies the risk of the strategy as well as creating risk by giving the lender power over the disposition of the investment portfolio. This may occur in the form of increased margin requirements or adverse market shifts, forcing a partial or complete liquidation of the portfolio.

◆ **Change in strategy.** Shifting course certainly undercuts the meaningfulness of past performance, and if the investment has already been made, the basis for investing might no longer exist. It is often a symptom of some of the other issues discussed in this section.

◆ **Exceeding stated risk parameters.** This development often indicates a problem with the strategy or manager capacity.

◆ **Character/ego.** Personality flaws can blind or cloud the thinking of a manager, resulting in a conscious deviation from prudent money management activities.

◆ **Fraud.** Direct fraud is not common and can be weeded out through proper due diligence. Be on the lookout for more subtle misrepresentation and material omissions, as these are commonplace.

TRANSPARENCY

TRANSPARENCY IS THE ability to look through a hedge fund to its investment portfolio. Transparency is essential in determining whether the fund complies with and adheres to the fund's stated investment and risk parameters and other representations made to the investor.

Investors want to be assured that they are getting the exposure and type of investment that they believe the manager sold them. This is particularly important to those with fiduciary responsibilities for investing others' assets. In reality, many managers tend to promote a more specific investment strategy than their funds actually pursue. Most investors are aware that blind faith creates a foolhardy investment strategy. Without transparency, they can only determine actual risk exposure and risk/reward prospects from secondary sources. As discussed in Chapter 15, prudent investing requires an investigation of the specifics of a fund manager's investment strategy, past performance, and the risk controls used to achieve the fund's returns. Based on this information, the investor constructs a set of future expectations for performance and risk parameters to which the manager must adhere. Parameters include use of leverage, types of instruments used, exposure to asset classes and sectors, number of positions, position size, amount of hedging, and frequency of trades. For each strategy, the investor should develop general parameters, and for each manager within that strategy there should be additional, more refined, parameters. Transparency ensures that the fund or the manager can be monitored for parameter compliance.

With transparency, the risk exposures of a hedge fund investment as well as a multiple fund or manager allocation can be monitored continuously by screening the portfolio on a daily basis for compliance with the parameters established during the initial due diligence process. This approach allows the investor to ensure conformity to investment guidelines. If a parameter is breached, the violation is detected, allowing it to be addressed immediately.

The portfolio is analyzed in three ways: 1 exposures, 2 relationships, and 3 time series. An exposure is a snapshot view of the portfolio's contents. Exposures are analyzed to determine portfolio position concentrations, how many are long positions and how many are short, and how much leverage is being used. The second level analyzed is the relationship between the instruments: not just how much of the portfolio is long and how much short, but the relationship between the longs and the shorts. Are they matched pairs? Are they iterative constructions? Are the short positions hedges against the long? Against the market? An example of this would be the relationship between a long position and a Standard and Poor's put-spread taken to hedge against catastrophic market decline. Time series analysis examines time-dependent variables such as duration, time horizons of particular positions, and cyclical features. An example of this would be the average length of time a position is held in a risk-arbitrage portfolio.

Investors use risk monitoring to confirm that each fund manager complies with the established risk parameters on a daily basis. For investors whose portfolios are allocated to more than a style manager, risk monitoring can be used to oversee the preset risk exposure of the multiple-manager composite. It allows investors to monitor whether their portfolio is diversified and risk exposure reduced, as would be expected when investment strategies are combined.

Technologies that allow for cost-effective risk monitoring are now available, and these can be provided to investors who are afforded transparency by the managers with whom they invest.

ILLUSTRATION OF DAILY RISK MONITORING

THE FOLLOWING IS a step-by-step illustration of how the risk-monitoring process works. The basis for this example is the methodologies and systems developed by and used at Hedge Fund Research, L.L.C. Once allocations are made, the portfolio is monitored daily for risk, performance, and administrative purposes. Risk monitoring involves three processes: portfolio valuation, compliance analysis, and reporting.

PORTFOLIO VALUATION

FOR EACH INVESTMENT manager who is represented in the portfolio, the previous day's transactions, portfolio holdings, and account activities are downloaded directly from the prime broker, counterparty, or custodian with which each investment manager books trades and maintains an account. This is important because the information must come from a third party, not the manager.

Repricing is absolutely necessary. Broker pricing is often inaccurate or incomplete. In many cases, the portfolio is priced by the manager. Obviously, there has to be an independent review. Prices should be confirmed for every instrument in the portfolio by using information provided by an independent pricing data source. Closing exchange rates should be obtained to convert any securities priced in non–dollar-denominated assets for purposes of risk analysis and portfolio valuation. In the event that a current market price is not available for a particular security, the risk monitor should obtain market pricing information from third-party sources such as market makers, brokers, and dealers. Theoretically priced instruments such as collateralized mortgage obligations, swaps, and repurchase agreements are valued by using an industry standard model. Accrued interest can be calculated using standard calculation methods developed by the Securities Industry Association. At the conclusion of the last trade day of each month, a final confirmation and validation of market price, quantity, and market value of each investment in the account is conducted. In addition, fees and fee accruals for each account are confirmed with each fund manager.

COMPLIANCE ANALYSIS

WHEN THE PORTFOLIO valuation process is complete, each investment manager is assessed for compliance with the risk parameters that were established for the portfolio. Every risk parameter is checked against the account's holdings, transactions, and activity. Compliance with each parameter is documented daily in a guideline summary report. This report identifies each risk parameter and indicates whether the parameter was violated.

Every investment parameter violation will undergo an analysis on a daily basis to determine its severity. Levels of violation severity are classified to designate which violations require further investigation and/or action and specify the course of corrective action to be taken. Each violation is assigned a severity level based on previously determined risk parameters. If the violation adversely affects the risk and/or performance of the account, then the violation will be assigned a higher severity level. For a multiple–hedge fund portfolio, the following severity levels might be established:

LEVEL ONE

◆ **Definition.** Any non–risk-increasing violation, or any instance in which a parameter is within 5 percent of being met and not otherwise determined to be a material violation or to materially increase risk (i.e., under-investment).

◆ **Action.** The violation is documented, and the violating investment manager is placed on a watch list. If the violation represents a nonmaterial increase in risk rather than a non–risk-reducing violation, the manager will be notified and the violation will be investigated within two business days. Other level one violations will be addressed with the investment managers within a reasonable period of time if these violations persist.

LEVEL TWO

◆ **Definition.** Parameter violation of 5 to 10 percent that increases risk.

◆ **Action.** The violation is documented, and the investment manager is contacted to investigate the violation within one business day.

LEVEL THREE

◆ **Definition.** Parameter violation exceeding 10 percent, or any account activity not specifically permitted in the guidelines, or any material increase in risk.

◆ **Action.** Both the investment manager and the prime broker are notified immediately to investigate violations. Corrective action may include, but is not limited to, liquidation, position offset, and reallocation of the non-compliant investment manager's assets and removal of the investment manager from the portfolio. The client is notified within five business days of the violation and of the resultant corrective action.

Each parameter violation is ranked according to severity levels custom-designed for the portfolio. All violations are listed on the daily guideline summary report, and the appropriate level is indicated. All parameter violations are documented and investigated, and corrective action is taken as specified by preset procedures.

REPORTING PROCEDURES

THE FOLLOWING MONITORING reports are typical:

1 **Daily guideline summary report.** This daily report lists each risk parameter for each investment manager, specifies the account's activity in relation to the parameter, and indicates whether the parameter was violated. The report also shows the ranking for each violated parameter.

2 **Daily valuation summary.** This daily report provides the accurate value of the account, by both investment manager and overall portfolio. Manager summaries itemize each manager's holdings by value of long, short, and cash positions. If valuations change for a particular account in subsequent days, a corrected report reflecting these changes is provided.

3 **Monthly and quarterly performance reports.** Performance reports detail each investment manager's performance as well as the overall performance of the portfolio.

4 **Customized reports.** These reports are tailored to address parameters specific to a particular client or portfolio.

SUMMARY POINTS

◆ Due diligence is an ongoing process.
◆ Factors and representations from the due diligence process form the basis for investment activity and performance expectations.
◆ Managers and funds are selected based on these expectations.
◆ If the factors change or the representations are not met, the expectations may change and, in turn, the basis for the invest-

ment with the fund or manager may no longer exist.

◆ Therefore, qualitative factors should be reviewed periodically and investment activities and portfolio exposures should be monitored on a daily basis for compliance with the risk parameters.

Epilogue
THE FUTURE OF HEDGE FUNDS

HE HEDGE FUND industry will surely continue to expand and evolve. The information technologies and computerization that help drive the industry continue to develop and global markets continue to expand. Significant market events, such as the collapse of the Russian markets, international liquidity crises, and stock market corrections, have resulted in gains and losses by various hedge fund strategies that make plain some of the latent benefits and risks of hedge fund investing.

Each year certain funds that secretly take excessive risks, such as Long Term Capital, will post significant losses. Investors will learn from these events, altering their strategy allocation choices and increasing their demand for information with which to make decisions.

The standard for prudent investing will require transparency at the investment instrument level as well as the establishment of risk parameters and a monitoring of these exposures. Investors will focus on the specific risk and return characteristics of the individual hedge fund strategies rather than evaluating hedge funds as a group. While the trend towards growth in the hedge fund industry remains in place, industry components such as types of structures, and strategy compositions, and weightings will change as much, if not more, in the next ten years as they have in the last decade. We will discuss some important trends in this epilogue.

INVESTORS

THE NUMBER AND VARIETY of hedge fund investors will continue to increase. This trend will be driven by increased awareness and education about hedge fund strategies and the availability of more investment products targeted at specific investor requirements. As the information gap narrows, investors will understand the range of investment opportunities available and will select strategies that best suit their needs.

The number of institutional investors and the percentage of the hedge fund assets they represent will increase gradually, but their impact will be significant. These assets will be concentrated in strategies that are specialized, categorized, and indexed, so that their exposures and performance can be monitored and measured. Prudent investing will require full transparency. Institutional participation will result in more disciplined and well-defined money management operations with a high level of accountability. Existing money management operations will be modified and new operations will be created to provide access to information in a manner acceptable to institutional investors; transparency of investment activities, risk controls, and increased reporting and accountability will become the norm.

The number of individual investors will also increase as they become better informed about the various strategies, and as they find more information and a broader variety of single-manager and multiple-manager products available.

MULTIPLE MANAGER FUNDS

THE MULTIPLE MANAGER and fund of funds business will also expand, funneling additional assets to hedge funds. Large institutions with traditional retail distribution channels will act as packagers of strategies to meet the growing individual demand for access to the broad range of investment opportunities provided by hedge fund strategies. Some of these will be in a mutual fund format designed to tap a broad base of investors.

HEDGE FUND MANAGERS

NEW MANAGERS WILL CONTINUE to emerge to exploit both new and established investment niches. Most will be investor oriented, providing access to their investment portfolios as well as organized reporting and client service.

Many will register as investment advisers, concentrating on institutional investors, which will require a high level of reporting and accountability.

Existing managers will have to decide how to deal with growth and business expansion. Some will become more institutionally oriented; others will close their doors to new allocations and remain small.

For new managers entering the industry, the barriers to entry are still relatively low in terms of start-up costs. But, a separation will occur as certain managers build infrastructures to handle increased growth and meet the needs of sophisticated and institutional investors.

The hedge fund industry is converging with the mainstream investing industry as large traditional money managers expand product lines to include hedge fund strategies. Some of these products will be internally developed, while other traditional money management operations will lure individuals from the hedge fund industry or acquire existing hedge fund businesses.

STRUCTURES

REGULATORY AND TRADITIONAL barriers that have kept hedge funds separate from traditional investments have begun to fall, allowing hedge fund strategies to be accessed by investors through traditional investment vehicles such as mutual funds. Other levels of regulation may develop, but the trend seems to favor the absorption of much of the hedge fund activity into traditional structures, which already have significant regulatory oversight.

The fees that different funds charge will become more stratified based on strategy and capacity. Already, certain strategies are available with reduced or nonincentive-based compensation. Managers who operate similar strategies will have to justify higher fees. Access to particular information increases an understanding of the risk component of many managers and allows returns to be normalized. On the other hand, many managers operating strategies that are more specialized with capacity constraints will have less incentive to reduce fees.

Hedge funds will make more information available about their investment activities, including risk and exposure reports. Large individual and institutional investors alike agree that the prudent way to invest requires transparency, risk control, and oversight. A growing number of investors will require that the portfolio underlying their hedge fund investments be independently priced and monitored. The majority of hedge fund mangers seeking investors will become partially or fully transparent.

STRATEGIES

NEW STRATEGIES AND sub-strategies will be introduced to take advantage of opportunities presented by new markets, instruments, and technologies.

Investment management operations with larger capacities will develop, often housing multiple strategies. These will include traditional money managers, banks, and brokerage firms that provide an investing, risk control, and client service platform.

Increased transparency and information flow means that strategies will become better defined and more specialized, providing greater differentiation and more exposure options for investors. Investors, in turn, will more specifically target sources of return and exposures in their portfolios.

The industry weightings in the various strategies will change, favoring more hedged and so-called "market-neutral" approaches. The broader base of both institutional and individual investors will be interested in more consistent performance and hedged exposures with returns in the low to mid-teens range. While there will still be plenty of interest in more aggressive strategies offering potential for higher returns, the composition of asset weighting in the industry will continue to shift toward the more conservative strategies.

INVESTING

HEDGE FUNDS INVESTING will become increasing more like traditional investing. The various strategies will, one by one, become part of the general investment universe and will be considered based on their specific exposure and risk/reward characteristics. The availability of information about funds, managers, and their investment portfolios will continue to increase, making them more accessible to a broader base of investors. More detailed information about investment activities (transparency) will allow for improved strategy classifications, greater delineation among substrategies, and better benchmarks, allowing investors to be more precise in their fund and manager selections. Finally, investors will have a greater choice of investment products as hedge fund strategies become available in mutual funds, separate accounts, and unit trust structures.

PERFORMANCE

AFTER A NUMBER of years of strong results, several hedge fund strategies witnessed extremely poor performance in a few months in 1998. Investors experienced the risks of leverage, illiquid markets and blind investments. However many strategies performed well relative to the declines in the U.S. equity markets. Monthly performance for the strategy indices from January 1990 through December 2001 are included in Appendix C. Ongoing monthly updates are available at **WWW.HFR.COM**.

APPENDICES

APPENDIX A

CALCULATION METHODOLOGY

THE RELEVANCE OF any performance index is its ability to gauge objectively market movement so that it may be used as a benchmark for various investment styles. In particular, when using an index such as the Standard and Poor's (S&P) 500 or the Dow Jones Industrial Average, it is important to understand the construction of these indices. It would seem inappropriate to use the S&P 500 as a benchmark for an investment firm that concentrates on small-cap equities, just as it would be inappropriate to use the Dow Jones Industrial Average as a benchmark for a firm that invests in corporate debt. I believe that it is inaccurate to compare hedge fund performance only with passive indices such as the S&P 500.

All statistics included in this book were compiled by Hedge Fund Research, Inc. (HFR). HFR has created an index of hedge fund performance categorized by investment strategy. The HFR Performance Indices (HFRI) is an equal-weighted summary of more than 2,000 hedge funds, categorized by 27 investment strategies (including specific indices for prominent sectors and emerging markets) and as a final composite index. These indices retain performance of liquidated funds over the life span of the funds, eliminating survivor bias. The strategies covered in this book were chosen because they represent the majority of this universe of funds in terms of both quantity and assets under management.

Each strategy is reweighted every month based on the number of funds that have provided their monthly performance. For example, if ten market neutral funds reported their performance for January, each fund's performance would be given ¹⁄₁₀ weight for January. If fourteen funds report in February, each of these funds would then be given ¹⁄₁₄ weight for

February. The statistics provided in this book are based on the monthly performance of the respective indices. Each statistic is calculated over the time period spanning January 1990 to March 1998. The minimum requirement for inclusion in an index is $5 million under management.

DEFINITIONS

Average gain. The average percentage gain in periods with a positive return.

Average loss. The average percentage loss in periods with a negative return.

Beta. A measure of how much the value of a security or portfolio of securities moves in relation to the average performance of the stock market for a given period of time. In this book, beta is calculated by comparing the price movements of the HFRI indices with the S&P 500 index of blue-chip stocks.

Gain period. The percentage of periods with positive or neutral returns.

High-period return. The highest rate of return for a one-month time period.

Low-period return. The lowest rate of return for a one-month time period.

Maximum drawdown. The peak-to-valley percentage change in the value of some initial investment in a fund.

One-period arithmetic standard deviation. The distribution of performance over any single time period (one month) for a given set of noncompounded returns.

One-period geometric average. The hypothetical rate of return for a single time period (one month), derived from the compounded geometric return of a time series.

Risk-free interest rate. The 3-month U.S. Treasury bill rate used in calculating the Sharpe ratio. The statistics in this book assume a 5 percent risk-free rate.

Sharpe ratio. The reward-to-risk ratio, discounting for the risk-free interest rate. It is calculated as follows: Annualized geometric performance – Risk-free interest rate annual standard deviation.

APPENDIX B

RESOURCES FOR INVESTORS

CONSULTING SERVICES

Salomon Smith Barney Consulting Group   302-888-4125
222 Delaware Avenue, 9th Floor
Wilmington, DE 19801

Lynx Investment Advisors, Inc.   202-833-3700
1100 Connecticut Avenue, NW
Washington, DC 20036

HEDGE FUND INVESTMENTS

HFR Asset Management   312-327-0430
10 South Riverside Plaza, Suite 1450   www.hfram.com
Chicago, IL 60606

Barclays Capital   44-20-7623-2323
5 The North Colonnade   www.barcap.com
London E14 4BB
United Kingdom

Wells Fargo Alternative Asset Management   415-222-4000
420 Montgomery Street, 5th Floor
San Francisco, CA 94104

DATABASE AND ANALYSIS SOFTWARE

Strategic Financial Solutions, LLC (Pertrac)   901-748-3043
8275 Tournament Drive, Suite 100   www.pertrac.com
Memphis, TN 38125-8899

Standard & Poor's Fund Services (Micropal)   44-20-8938-7100
Commonwealth House   www.sp-funds.com
2 Chalkhill Road
London W6 8DW
United Kingdom

Zephyr Associates, Inc. (StyleADVISOR)   775-588-0654
P.O. Box 12368   www.styleadvisor.com
Zephyr Cove, NV 89448

Burlington Hall Asset Management (La Porte)   908-813-0077
43-A Newburgh Road, Suite 200   www.laportesoft.com
Hackettstown, NJ 07840

ASSOCIATIONS

Managed Funds Association   202-367-1140
2025 M Street NW, Suite 800   www.mfainfo.org
Washington, DC 20036

Alternative Investment Management   44-20-7659-9920
   Association (AIMA)   www.aima.org
Lower Ground Floor, 10 Stanhope Gate
London W1K 1AL
United Kingdom

APPENDIX C

HEDGE FUND RESEARCH PERFORMANCE INDICES

FUND	# OF FUNDS	AVG SIZE (MM)	YEAR	JAN	FEB	MAR
Convertible Arbitrage	4		1990	-1.47	-0.92	1.26
Convertible Arbitrage	7		1991	0.44	1.61	1.39
Convertible Arbitrage	11	7	1992	2.12	0.94	0.99
Convertible Arbitrage	22	14	1993	0.93	0.86	2.19
Convertible Arbitrage	27	20	1994	0.66	0.24	-2.11
Convertible Arbitrage	32	21	1995	0.55	0.98	1.83
Convertible Arbitrage	33	28	1996	1.82	1.06	1.17
Convertible Arbitrage	35	60	1997	1.01	1.11	0.59
Convertible Arbitrage	40	67	1998	1.91	1.52	1.58
Convertible Arbitrage	48	97	1999	2.11	0.25	1.53
Convertible Arbitrage	53	140	2000	1.91	2.21	1.75
Convertible Arbitrage	62	152	2001	2.73	1.70	1.68
Distressed Securities	8	20	1990	-0.24	2.79	3.08
Distressed Securities	13	24	1991	2.00	4.14	6.84
Distressed Securities	14	33	1992	7.06	5.45	2.32
Distressed Securities	18	44	1993	4.50	2.54	3.14
Distressed Securities	27	39	1994	3.82	-0.30	-0.93
Distressed Securities	38	44	1995	1.08	2.08	1.56
Distressed Securities	41	56	1996	2.22	1.43	2.18
Distressed Securities	44	73	1997	1.88	1.84	0.22
Distressed Securities	41	99	1998	1.10	2.35	2.17
Distressed Securities	42	119	1999	1.40	-0.27	2.20
Distressed Securities	39	113	2000	0.70	3.98	0.67
Distressed Securities	47	123	2001	2.79	1.30	-0.62
Emerging Markets (Total)	5		1990	-0.84	2.06	0.63
Emerging Markets (Total)	8		1991	2.43	8.19	4.16
Emerging Markets (Total)	14	265	1992	8.06	3.26	2.77
Emerging Markets (Total)	29	179	1993	3.69	6.29	4.07
Emerging Markets (Total)	57	130	1994	5.32	-0.56	-4.38
Emerging Markets (Total)	81	105	1995	-5.50	-2.17	-0.71
Emerging Markets (Total)	104	78	1996	5.69	-1.62	0.09
Emerging Markets (Total)	112	109	1997	7.83	5.92	-1.48
Emerging Markets (Total)	117	102	1998	-5.43	3.96	2.94
Emerging Markets (Total)	115	73	1999	-2.32	1.54	8.86

APR	MAY	JUN	JUL	AUG	SEP	OCT	NOV	DEC	ANNUAL
1.48	1.75	1.72	1.15	-0.18	-0.47	-1.56	-0.05	-0.49	2.16
1.49	0.94	0.98	1.57	2.09	1.31	1.22	1.66	1.63	17.60
0.80	1.70	0.71	1.85	1.65	1.46	1.24	0.70	1.09	16.35
1.50	1.24	1.04	1.41	1.40	1.03	1.29	0.60	0.77	15.22
-2.79	0.03	0.15	1.55	0.80	0.12	-0.09	-0.79	-1.48	-3.73
1.90	1.88	2.32	2.13	0.96	1.55	1.25	1.58	1.33	19.85
1.88	1.73	0.44	-0.37	1.40	1.23	1.27	1.40	0.66	14.56
0.68	1.40	1.71	1.61	1.14	1.11	1.19	0.09	0.41	12.72
1.35	0.40	0.22	0.49	-3.19	-1.07	-0.48	3.33	1.60	7.77
2.66	1.40	1.09	1.05	0.42	0.66	0.33	0.99	1.08	14.41
1.78	1.34	1.66	0.68	1.42	1.21	0.42	-0.71	-0.01	14.50
1.57	0.71	0.13	0.76	1.26	0.63	0.91	0.57	0.11	13.50
0.65	0.82	3.65	2.02	-1.90	-3.58	-2.86	1.00	1.12	6.44
5.33	1.36	1.72	3.18	1.37	1.91	2.02	0.39	0.83	35.66
0.32	1.13	-0.01	0.27	0.89	0.93	0.12	1.66	2.84	25.24
1.63	2.23	2.71	2.99	2.52	0.70	1.97	0.87	2.76	32.54
-0.15	0.38	-0.45	1.13	1.20	0.40	0.42	-1.71	0.07	3.84
1.83	1.24	2.06	2.31	1.34	2.09	-0.09	1.14	1.53	19.73
3.06	2.07	1.35	0.21	1.73	1.82	0.95	0.88	1.15	20.77
0.07	1.74	1.89	2.11	1.08	2.84	-0.20	0.69	0.30	15.40
1.55	0.28	0.13	-0.40	-8.50	-3.57	-0.75	1.70	0.15	-4.23
5.06	1.91	1.93	0.68	0.37	-1.00	-0.15	1.14	2.62	16.94
-1.43	-0.78	2.31	0.26	1.29	-0.44	-0.85	-2.49	-0.31	2.78
0.18	2.75	3.09	0.79	0.68	-0.37	0.84	1.34	0.81	14.37
-1.87	6.57	1.88	5.88	-12.07	-6.71	4.82	-2.19	0.03	-3.35
1.94	2.51	-1.17	5.43	0.79	-0.03	0.37	1.89	12.27	45.40
1.39	4.13	-3.74	-0.47	-2.01	3.41	3.28	0.31	2.12	24.35
5.02	5.58	4.59	0.86	5.63	2.57	7.84	3.95	9.99	79.22
-2.36	0.45	-0.55	3.17	7.87	3.21	-2.09	-2.81	-3.17	3.38
2.81	3.69	1.24	1.58	0.25	1.07	-2.66	-1.47	2.96	0.69
5.04	4.27	3.88	-2.65	2.42	1.38	1.48	2.85	1.78	27.14
1.59	3.80	6.41	4.64	-2.08	0.61	-7.96	-3.92	1.27	16.57
-0.55	-9.32	-6.01	-0.30	-21.02	-4.98	2.16	5.14	-2.76	-32.96
7.45	0.47	9.34	-0.99	-1.45	-1.89	3.13	7.90	14.80	55.86

FUND	# OF FUNDS	AVG SIZE (MM)	YEAR	JAN	FEB	MAR
Emerging Markets (Total)	103	44	2000	0.20	4.80	3.38
Emerging Markets (Total)	85	44	2001	6.61	-2.71	-3.07
Equity Hedge	12	44	1990	-3.34	2.85	5.67
Equity Hedge	26	48	1991	4.90	5.20	7.22
Equity Hedge	37	33	1992	2.49	2.90	-0.28
Equity Hedge	59	29	1993	2.09	-0.57	3.26
Equity Hedge	78	42	1994	2.35	-0.40	-2.08
Equity Hedge	90	41	1995	0.30	1.68	2.09
Equity Hedge	102	70	1996	1.06	2.82	1.90
Equity Hedge	133	76	1997	2.78	-0.24	-0.73
Equity Hedge	227	100	1998	-0.16	4.09	4.54
Equity Hedge	275	131	1999	4.98	-2.41	4.05
Equity Hedge	291	141	2000	0.25	10.00	1.73
Equity Hedge	345	132	2001	2.88	-2.56	-2.30
Equity Market Neutral	8	14	1990	1.23	1.23	0.82
Equity Market Neutral	10	19	1991	2.51	0.04	2.70
Equity Market Neutral	15	22	1992	0.36	0.96	0.58
Equity Market Neutral	19	22	1993	1.91	1.06	1.67
Equity Market Neutral	25	89	1994	0.78	0.58	0.44
Equity Market Neutral	31	75	1995	0.22	1.42	1.77
Equity Market Neutral	34	70	1996	2.18	0.95	0.86
Equity Market Neutral	38	133	1997	1.20	0.12	0.43
Equity Market Neutral	40	136	1998	0.54	0.76	1.26
Equity Market Neutral	42	155	1999	0.15	-1.33	-0.76
Equity Market Neutral	42	183	2000	-1.19	2.26	0.48
Equity Market Neutral	60	175	2001	-1.57	2.07	1.77
Equity Non-Hedge	18	5	1990	-5.07	1.66	4.50
Equity Non-Hedge	26	20	1991	4.91	9.31	9.58
Equity Non-Hedge	40	32	1992	5.44	2.30	-2.05
Equity Non-Hedge	52	45	1993	2.30	-1.49	3.77
Equity Non-Hedge	75	41	1994	3.17	-1.22	-3.07
Equity Non-Hedge	101	29	1995	0.33	3.24	3.34
Equity Non-Hedge	121	33	1996	2.12	3.36	2.79
Equity Non-Hedge	163	82	1997	3.39	-1.08	-5.04
Equity Non-Hedge	131	103	1998	-0.88	5.69	3.98
Equity Non-Hedge	104	118	1999	3.65	-3.84	2.87
Equity Non-Hedge	80	86	2000	-1.56	9.41	2.36
Equity Non-Hedge	67	82	2001	8.00	-7.41	-5.05
Event-Driven	13	32	1990	-5.69	1.69	4.92
Event-Driven	18	44	1991	1.00	4.42	3.37
Event-Driven	25	55	1992	4.21	2.13	1.59
Event-Driven	31	72	1993	3.07	1.63	3.85

APR	MAY	JUN	JUL	AUG	SEP	OCT	NOV	DEC	ANNUAL
-6.59	-5.05	3.11	-0.38	3.17	-5.53	-3.28	-5.50	1.35	-10.71
1.56	2.62	1.34	-3.22	0.18	-5.52	3.13	5.37	4.85	10.82
-0.87	5.92	2.52	2.00	-1.88	1.65	0.77	-2.29	1.02	14.43
0.47	3.20	0.59	1.41	2.17	4.30	1.16	-1.08	5.02	40.15
0.27	0.85	-0.92	2.76	-0.85	2.51	2.03	4.51	3.38	21.32
1.30	2.72	3.01	2.12	3.84	2.52	3.11	-1.93	3.59	27.94
-0.37	0.41	-0.41	0.91	1.27	1.32	0.40	-1.48	0.74	2.61
2.64	1.22	4.73	4.46	2.93	2.90	-1.44	3.43	2.56	31.04
5.34	3.70	-0.73	-2.87	2.63	2.18	1.56	1.66	0.83	21.75
-0.27	5.04	1.97	5.05	1.35	5.69	0.39	-0.93	1.42	23.41
1.39	-1.27	0.50	-0.67	-7.65	3.16	2.47	3.84	5.39	15.98
5.25	1.22	3.80	0.61	0.04	0.35	2.33	6.76	10.88	44.22
-4.19	-2.44	4.85	-1.58	5.35	-1.08	-2.01	-4.30	3.16	9.09
2.27	0.90	-0.32	-1.06	-1.22	-3.63	1.77	1.81	2.09	0.37
0.73	0.50	1.37	0.77	1.80	1.81	1.37	0.83	2.01	15.45
-0.01	-0.02	0.56	2.50	0.28	1.92	0.97	1.17	2.07	15.65
-0.03	0.11	0.62	1.24	-0.35	1.17	1.04	1.18	1.54	8.73
-0.14	0.58	2.37	0.63	0.91	2.44	-0.10	-1.45	0.77	11.11
0.92	-0.95	0.58	0.37	-0.35	0.02	-0.12	-0.45	0.82	2.65
1.86	0.60	0.92	2.23	0.98	1.85	1.58	0.78	1.03	16.33
0.35	1.39	1.37	1.62	0.78	0.66	2.10	0.16	0.95	14.20
0.96	1.49	1.54	2.17	0.21	2.18	1.36	0.53	0.67	13.62
0.66	0.48	1.69	-0.27	-1.67	0.81	-0.61	0.85	3.59	8.30
-0.65	0.17	2.02	1.91	0.70	0.85	0.44	1.05	2.39	7.09
2.64	0.27	1.50	-0.04	3.06	0.94	0.23	1.03	2.58	14.56
0.06	0.28	0.36	0.45	1.73	1.31	-0.28	-0.49	0.60	6.41
-3.09	7.43	1.99	-0.76	-10.66	-6.13	-2.20	4.16	2.25	-7.17
0.28	4.56	-2.52	4.83	3.84	2.23	3.85	-2.32	8.33	57.07
-2.31	1.19	-2.90	3.67	-1.65	2.59	4.81	6.93	3.28	22.78
-0.26	5.23	1.44	2.21	4.38	1.97	3.65	-2.22	3.80	27.42
-0.41	0.71	-0.95	2.50	4.81	0.22	0.90	-2.43	1.04	5.10
2.46	1.89	4.83	6.52	3.11	3.02	-2.35	2.64	1.47	34.80
7.50	5.40	2.62	-6.79	3.88	3.97	-0.51	2.96	1.68	25.52
-0.54	8.98	3.19	5.56	0.86	6.36	-2.67	-1.47	-0.34	17.56
1.43	-2.77	1.02	-2.87	-13.34	3.44	3.98	6.64	4.80	9.80
6.36	1.10	4.77	0.53	-1.16	-0.62	2.66	9.37	10.74	41.82
-8.36	-4.83	7.17	-2.74	7.35	-4.31	-5.15	-8.43	1.73	-9.04
5.71	2.32	0.04	-2.36	-3.08	-8.32	4.54	4.48	3.47	0.73
1.16	1.93	1.37	1.14	-4.53	-2.78	-1.60	0.80	1.63	-0.47
3.06	2.85	0.24	2.33	1.26	1.48	2.34	0.52	1.69	27.42
0.33	1.01	0.11	1.22	0.24	1.36	0.96	1.71	3.12	19.46
1.21	1.88	2.99	2.10	2.79	0.87	1.68	0.16	2.95	28.22

FUND	# OF FUNDS	AVG SIZE (MM)	YEAR	JAN	FEB	MAR
Event-Driven	37	89	1994	3.51	-0.49	-0.55
Event-Driven	49	91	1995	2.04	1.27	0.69
Event-Driven	58	89	1996	3.89	1.45	1.88
Event-Driven	68	127	1997	2.84	0.93	-0.53
Event-Driven	61	140	1998	0.25	3.36	2.93
Event-Driven	58	170	1999	1.65	-0.48	2.06
Event-Driven	68	176	2000	0.74	3.76	0.03
Event-Driven	67	203	2001	4.59	-0.38	-0.25
Fixed Income: Arbitrage	4	35	1990	2.25	2.10	-0.21
Fixed Income: Arbitrage	4	37	1991	4.00	2.42	1.52
Fixed Income: Arbitrage	5	43	1992	4.70	2.53	2.53
Fixed Income: Arbitrage	9	56	1993	0.25	0.89	1.47
Fixed Income: Arbitrage	13	97	1994	2.32	1.63	0.93
Fixed Income: Arbitrage	21	99	1995	0.64	0.34	1.79
Fixed Income: Arbitrage	24	115	1996	0.95	0.69	0.58
Fixed Income: Arbitrage	23	130	1997	1.43	1.17	0.54
Fixed Income: Arbitrage	22	141	1998	0.39	1.28	1.34
Fixed Income: Arbitrage	19	101	1999	1.17	1.09	1.31
Fixed Income: Arbitrage	12	143	2000	-0.67	1.31	-1.35
Fixed Income: Arbitrage	15	102	2001	2.17	0.41	-0.44
Fund of Funds	19	27	1990	0.07	1.34	2.07
Fund of Funds	33	163	1991	0.39	-0.03	3.52
Fund of Funds	51	195	1992	1.32	1.16	0.80
Fund of Funds	79	258	1993	0.87	2.20	1.51
Fund of Funds	112	180	1994	1.26	-2.27	-2.31
Fund of Funds	157	97	1995	-1.26	-0.09	1.43
Fund of Funds	169	84	1996	2.73	-0.62	0.99
Fund of Funds	187	107	1997	3.55	1.68	-0.82
Fund of Funds	209	98	1998	-0.96	1.90	4.01
Fund of Funds	226	91	1999	1.41	-0.22	2.08
Fund of Funds	211	107	2000	1.54	5.21	0.23
Fund of Funds	224	104	2001	1.93	-0.74	-0.44
Macro	7	592	1990	-1.23	0.48	3.54
Macro	10	595	1991	-0.25	6.31	6.85
Macro	13	654	1992	2.80	0.34	0.32
Macro	19	1,105	1993	0.91	5.17	5.54
Macro	23	769	1994	2.11	-6.40	-3.43
Macro	30	567	1995	-0.87	1.45	1.40
Macro	34	408	1996	5.28	-3.77	0.37
Macro	52	452	1997	5.14	1.59	-1.24
Macro	50	323	1998	0.20	1.90	5.05
Macro	47	331	1999	0.81	-1.24	1.07

APR	MAY	JUN	JUL	AUG	SEP	OCT	NOV	DEC	ANNUAL
-0.70	0.94	1.12	1.56	1.81	0.41	-0.40	-1.27	0.00	6.00
2.11	1.84	1.48	1.98	2.14	1.85	0.09	5.01	2.19	25.11
2.62	3.53	0.43	-0.50	2.42	1.97	0.97	2.03	1.78	24.84
-0.83	4.36	2.65	2.72	0.52	3.59	0.45	1.36	1.49	21.23
0.31	-1.19	0.31	-0.57	-8.90	-0.62	1.25	2.43	2.73	1.70
5.13	2.00	2.93	0.81	-0.78	1.62	0.42	3.38	3.39	24.33
-1.48	-0.77	2.92	0.15	2.01	0.63	-1.32	-2.32	2.39	6.74
1.23	1.94	1.11	0.30	1.29	-3.24	2.26	1.45	2.72	13.60
2.23	0.32	0.15	0.68	0.03	0.49	1.22	0.55	0.57	10.84
1.88	2.34	1.39	1.96	-0.82	-2.58	-0.03	-1.17	1.46	12.89
2.26	0.62	-0.45	-0.08	0.84	-0.79	3.33	2.18	2.62	22.11
1.45	1.94	0.37	1.99	1.50	0.70	0.96	2.12	1.87	16.64
0.98	0.75	1.32	0.36	0.71	0.88	0.65	0.76	0.06	11.94
0.64	-0.54	-1.18	2.49	0.92	-1.89	1.58	-0.01	1.22	6.08
1.39	1.15	1.35	1.30	0.63	0.52	1.18	-0.37	1.94	11.89
0.98	0.34	0.67	0.58	0.40	0.51	-0.37	-0.14	0.71	7.02
1.03	0.19	-1.31	1.69	-1.18	-6.45	-6.09	-1.42	0.15	-10.29
0.11	-0.03	1.32	0.65	-0.34	0.25	0.25	1.07	0.31	7.38
0.51	3.04	0.25	-1.02	1.83	0.46	-0.50	0.60	0.30	4.78
1.12	0.62	-0.48	0.16	1.13	-1.54	0.96	0.09	0.30	4.54
0.89	0.47	2.21	3.07	1.63	2.84	1.64	0.00	0.09	17.53
-0.83	0.77	1.18	0.51	1.31	1.76	0.61	0.05	4.50	14.50
0.12	0.28	0.44	0.82	0.47	2.49	1.70	0.30	1.81	12.33
2.30	2.07	2.75	2.43	1.79	0.33	2.26	0.40	4.76	26.32
-1.11	0.42	0.77	0.17	1.29	0.78	-0.95	-1.01	-0.49	-3.48
1.48	0.90	0.57	1.74	2.28	0.75	-0.53	1.15	2.22	11.10
3.09	1.54	0.38	-1.87	1.53	1.25	1.59	2.34	0.68	14.39
0.37	1.82	2.50	4.64	-0.32	2.78	-1.44	-0.51	1.05	16.20
0.91	-0.93	-0.55	-0.21	-7.47	-2.55	-1.96	1.44	1.60	-5.11
3.26	0.84	2.84	0.73	0.11	-0.12	1.27	4.91	6.85	26.47
-3.37	-1.58	2.82	-0.22	2.00	-1.16	-1.01	-1.54	1.38	4.07
0.69	0.90	-0.06	-0.43	0.18	-1.58	1.03	0.37	1.04	2.88
-0.74	3.98	1.65	3.83	-3.78	-0.98	2.60	1.14	1.71	12.56
-1.68	0.01	2.62	2.43	6.70	5.96	2.33	0.75	7.44	46.66
1.12	6.99	0.87	1.71	-1.06	2.28	4.66	3.13	1.37	27.17
2.69	2.99	7.15	3.71	3.71	-0.66	4.80	-0.01	7.88	53.31
-1.20	2.25	0.15	0.71	2.60	-0.12	-0.11	0.39	-0.98	-4.30
0.78	2.54	0.47	3.93	5.59	3.22	0.41	3.63	3.63	29.32
3.11	-0.08	-1.06	-3.04	0.73	2.01	1.58	4.72	-0.49	9.32
-0.22	1.83	1.82	5.90	-1.25	3.05	-1.60	-0.25	2.93	18.82
-0.13	0.08	0.57	0.23	-3.70	-0.50	-1.83	1.98	2.44	6.19
3.86	-0.90	2.16	0.46	-0.55	1.08	-0.75	3.83	6.82	17.62

FUND	# OF FUNDS	AVG SIZE (MM)	YEAR	JAN	FEB	MAR
Macro	44	255	2000	1.14	3.67	-2.27
Macro	42	110	2001	2.15	-1.71	0.83
Merger Arbitrage	7	5	1990	-6.46	1.71	2.90
Merger Arbitrage	8	5	1991	0.01	1.59	2.30
Merger Arbitrage	8	5	1992	1.96	0.96	1.34
Merger Arbitrage	10	5	1993	2.12	1.64	0.49
Merger Arbitrage	11	11	1994	1.50	-0.41	1.37
Merger Arbitrage	17	30	1995	0.86	1.45	1.49
Merger Arbitrage	20	41	1996	1.57	1.29	1.51
Merger Arbitrage	19	55	1997	1.04	0.39	1.05
Merger Arbitrage	28	61	1998	0.96	1.89	1.05
Merger Arbitrage	37	68	1999	0.71	0.25	1.05
Merger Arbitrage	44	105	2000	1.63	1.88	0.82
Merger Arbitrage	56	90	2001	1.10	0.44	-0.75
Sector (Total)	3	2	1990	-0.47	0.73	6.56
Sector (Total)	4	13	1991	5.70	4.50	1.21
Sector (Total)	12	9	1992	5.32	1.91	-0.09
Sector (Total)	19	13	1993	3.70	0.89	3.25
Sector (Total)	32	15	1994	2.57	-0.90	-1.28
Sector (Total)	52	13	1995	0.37	3.15	4.02
Sector (Total)	70	30	1996	5.14	2.88	1.72
Sector (Total)	76	65	1997	2.85	0.00	-4.53
Sector (Total)	80	151	1998	-1.34	3.67	2.18
Sector (Total)	74	103	1999	4.76	-3.62	6.37
Sector (Total)	99	110	2000	3.04	17.86	-4.32
Sector (Total)	114	64	2001	5.20	-8.97	-4.82
Short Selling	4		1990	9.15	2.16	0.91
Short Selling	6	1	1991	-3.97	-16.24	-2.19
Short Selling	8	2	1992	-2.78	-2.56	6.15
Short Selling	9	4	1993	-1.36	6.06	-3.41
Short Selling	12	11	1994	-4.87	0.98	11.32
Short Selling	12	13	1995	2.37	-2.06	-2.11
Short Selling	12	22	1996	0.09	-4.26	0.71
Short Selling	11	31	1997	-1.02	5.75	6.75
Short Selling	14	44	1998	1.33	-4.98	0.06
Short Selling	13	24	1999	-5.90	6.97	-0.04
Short Selling	12	22	2000	4.76	-21.21	1.04
Short Selling	12	26	2001	-1.89	11.77	7.14

PLEASE NOTE: Sept 01–Dec 01 are estimates

Criteria for a fund to be included in the HFR Monthly Indices:
• Fund must report "net of all fees" performance returns • Fund must report in $USD • Fund must report monthly
Other important notes concerning the HFR Monthly Indices:
• All HFRI are fund weighted (equal weighted). • There is no required asset-size minimum for fund inclusion in the HFRI.

APR	MAY	JUN	JUL	AUG	SEP	OCT	NOV	DEC	ANNUAL
-3.68	-1.54	1.24	0.05	1.73	-2.19	-0.73	0.25	4.61	1.97
-0.12	-0.10	0.43	-0.30	0.57	0.61	2.58	-0.09	2.92	7.95
0.98	2.28	0.73	0.02	-0.82	-4.58	0.73	2.19	1.21	0.44
2.83	1.55	1.12	1.44	0.64	1.10	1.41	1.38	1.20	17.86
0.14	0.00	0.30	1.45	0.12	1.34	0.40	-2.22	1.91	7.90
1.30	1.17	2.25	1.54	1.67	1.85	2.05	0.86	1.65	20.24
-0.25	1.22	0.89	0.68	1.99	0.59	-0.26	-0.22	1.48	8.88
0.35	1.26	2.47	1.35	1.35	1.63	0.91	2.13	1.31	17.86
1.62	1.46	0.78	0.81	1.64	0.81	1.23	1.38	1.37	16.61
-0.70	1.92	2.13	1.60	1.04	2.13	0.84	2.02	1.90	16.44
1.59	-0.60	0.50	-0.57	-5.69	1.74	2.14	2.33	1.94	7.23
1.31	2.04	1.61	1.38	0.52	1.25	0.69	2.23	0.46	14.34
2.47	1.51	1.58	1.19	1.34	1.44	0.48	1.20	1.16	18.02
0.23	1.69	-0.84	0.93	0.87	-2.79	0.85	0.21	0.72	2.61
1.30	-0.26	6.41	0.40	3.42	-2.43	3.66	5.21	4.08	32.09
0.64	1.21	-3.47	1.38	2.93	0.59	3.62	-1.49	4.78	23.40
1.04	3.65	-1.43	7.98	2.51	4.36	3.99	5.43	4.47	46.47
0.29	3.14	1.92	2.86	3.89	3.37	3.87	-0.74	3.09	33.71
-0.26	2.57	0.59	0.75	2.87	1.55	0.38	-2.08	1.08	7.98
3.10	1.94	4.60	5.47	4.83	2.48	1.46	2.95	2.62	39.65
4.72	4.13	-2.03	-2.54	3.97	3.27	0.62	3.12	2.39	30.68
-2.91	7.27	1.46	4.16	1.03	6.38	-2.79	-4.96	-1.96	5.21
2.48	-3.87	1.45	-2.32	-13.00	5.52	2.40	6.65	5.21	7.62
5.71	-0.06	5.62	1.00	3.04	0.35	3.70	10.42	16.53	67.00
-7.68	-5.89	10.50	-1.78	8.00	-2.84	-4.87	-10.34	2.29	0.31
5.17	1.20	0.47	-2.80	-3.79	-5.22	3.97	4.83	1.75	-4.20
5.15	-8.28	6.64	6.62	4.82	11.91	3.64	-7.68	-1.64	36.22
-0.76	-4.52	8.73	-0.66	-0.93	3.65	-0.59	8.83	-7.17	-16.96
7.64	1.86	7.80	-0.72	2.93	1.42	-4.21	-6.79	0.06	10.05
4.17	-9.19	0.16	3.35	-5.07	-2.54	-3.32	3.81	0.67	-7.50
3.33	2.28	12.04	-4.17	-6.48	0.52	0.43	4.70	-1.18	18.53
-0.16	-3.67	-9.96	-9.36	1.05	-0.65	7.66	-3.89	3.54	-17.14
-7.28	-2.82	9.26	9.00	-4.02	-7.53	6.47	-2.95	1.08	-4.00
-0.47	-8.23	-0.20	-2.94	-1.77	-2.58	4.60	2.21	2.69	3.86
-2.25	8.16	1.16	3.04	19.40	-4.18	-8.97	-4.84	-5.48	-0.54
-2.49	-0.20	-1.69	0.16	4.38	3.18	-3.17	-11.68	-14.60	-24.40
22.84	9.68	-11.38	7.30	-12.35	13.42	8.66	16.16	0.42	34.63
-12.03	-2.30	0.99	5.93	8.27	8.52	-2.49	-6.55	-4.03	10.99

• There is no required length of time a fund must be actively investing before inclusion in the HFRI. • Both onshore and offshore funds are included in the HFRI. • HFR does not reveal the underlying funds in the HFRI. • The current month and the previous three months are left as estimates and are subject to change. All performance prior to that is locked and is no longer subject to change. • The HFRI are updated 3 times a month (flash, mid, and end). • If a fund liquidates/closes, that fund's performance will be included in the HFRI as of that fund's last reported performance update.

GLOSSARY

Arbitrage. The simultaneous purchase and sale of a security or pair of similar securities to profit from a pricing discrepancy.

Boom-bust sequence. The process by which the value of an instrument or class of instruments is pushed to a valuation extreme, reverses itself, and crashes back to a more normal valuation.

Call feature. A feature that allows the issuer to redeem a bond before it matures.

Cash merger. A deal in which the acquiring company pays cash for the target company.

Catalyst. A near-term event, such as a press release or a new product launch, that will heighten investor interest in or change the market's perception of a company.

Catalytic event. A near-term event, such as a new product launch, that heightens investor interest in a company.

Collateral. Cash or very liquid securities that are held as a deposit on borrowed securities.

Conversion value. The value of a convertible bond if it were to be converted to common stock.

Convertible arbitrage. The simultaneous purchase of a convertible bond and sale of the common stock to profit from a pricing discrepancy.

Convertible bond. A corporate bond issued with a corporate bond yield and a conversion feature that allows the holder to convert the bond into a fixed number of shares of the issuing company's common stock.

Core positions. Long-term positions in growth stocks from which managers derive the majority of their profits.

Coupon. A bond's fixed interest payment.

Distressed securities. The securities of companies that are experiencing financial or operational difficulties. Distressed situations include reorganizations, bankruptcies, distressed sales, and other corporate restructurings.

Duration. A measure of how sensitive a bond's price is to a shift in interest rates. In general terms,

Duration = (Change in price)/Price
———————————————————
Change in interest rates

Emerging market. A market that is changing rapidly at the macro-economic and company level, usually because it is restructuring on the free market model.

Equity-market-neutral portfolio. A portfolio composed of balanced exposure to long stock positions and offsetting short stock positions.

Event analysis. The process by which an analyst assesses the probabilities of all the possible outcomes of a corporate event.

Exit catalyst. An event on the horizon that the distressed securities specialist expects to change the market's perception of, and therefore the value of, the distressed company.

Far-from-equilibrium condition. An unusual macro situation characterized by persistent price trends or extreme price valuations of particular financial instruments.

Fixed-income securities. Securities that entitle the holder to a series of fixed payments at predetermined future dates.

Fundamental value. The intrinsic or "real" value of a security, which reflects both tangible and intangible company assets.

Global investors. Investors who consider emerging markets to be one potential asset class, along with developed markets and fixed-income securities, and allocate capital to each asset class when they believe that it offers attractive potential returns compared with other asset classes.

Growth stock. A stock that an investor believes will appreciate because the company's output and earnings will grow.

Hedge ratio. The number of shares that the convertible arbitrage specialist decides to sell short out of the total number possible.

Hedging. The taking of positions to offset changes in economic conditions falling outside the core investment idea, such as purchasing a long position and a short position in similar stocks to offset the effect any changes in the overall level of the equity market will have on the long position.

Indicators. Financial data used to forecast the future performance of a company.

Inflection point. The point at which an extreme valuation reverses itself, usually marked or signaled by a major policy move.

Investment value. The value of the bond component of a convertible bond.

Leverage. The practice of borrowing to add to an investment position when one believes that the return from the position will exceed the cost of the borrowed funds. Both companies and investors can use leverage. A company that takes on more debt than its ability to generate cash warrants is said to be overleveraged.

Leveraged buy-out. An often hostile situation in which the acquiring company buys out the target company by using borrowed funds.

Liquidation. The sale of assets for cash, sometimes to pay off debt.

Mark to market. To determine the price one can get today for currently owned securities.

Market exposure. The amount of portfolio that is exposed to market risk because it is not matched by an offsetting position.

Market inefficiencies. Pricing disparities caused by a lack of information about a market or company or by a distortion of the information that is available.

Market-neutral portfolio. A portfolio composed of equal dollar amounts of long stock positions and offsetting short stock positions.

Maturity date. The date on which a bond is redeemed (a 5-year bond comes to maturity five years after it is issued).

Mortgage-backed securities. Securities that represent an ownership interest in mortgage loans made by financial institutions (such as savings and loans, commercial banks, or mortgage companies) to finance the borrower's purchase of a home.

Net market exposure. The percentage of the portfolio exposed to market fluctuations because long positions are not matched by equal dollar amounts of short positions. In general terms,

$$\text{Market exposure} = \frac{\text{Long exposure} - \text{Short exposure}}{\text{Capital}}$$

Overleveraged company. A company that has a large amount of debt relative to its ability to pay interest on that debt.

Par value. The face value of a bond, or the amount that it is redeemed for at maturity.

Prepayments. Payments to repay a mortgage loan ahead of the scheduled repayment date.

Relative value. The value of a particular security relative to that of other similar or related instruments, such as the same company's other debt instruments.

Sector. A group of companies or segment of the economy that is similar in either its product or its market, for example, health care, biotechnology, financial services, or information technologies.

Securities market infrastructure. The means of making investments and tracking financial information, including accounting standards, availability of trading and financial information, and sophistication of available financial instruments.

Senior debt. A class of debt securities whose holders a company is obligated to pay off before the holders of its other securities, in the case of bankruptcy.

Servicing debt. Paying the interest and principal due to bondholders.

Short interest rebate. The interest earned on the cash proceeds of a short sale of stock.

Short selling. The practice of borrowing a stock on collateral and immediately selling it on the market with the intention of buying it back later at a lower price.

Significant corporate events. Major public events, such as mergers, bankruptcies, and spin-offs, that have the potential to dramatically change a company's makeup and as a result the valuation of its debt and equity instruments.

Speculator. An investor who makes large directional bets on what financial markets will do next.

Spread. The difference between the prices of two comparable or related securities. Spreads are measured in basis points. One basis point equals 1/100 of a percent. For example, corporate bonds of a comparable maturity and comparable coupon rates will have higher yields than treasuries to reflect greater default risk, so their yields are often quoted as a spread above the Treasury rate. The more risky the bond issue, the larger is the spread.

Static return. Returns, such as interest income from coupon payments and short interest rebates from short sales of stock, that are unaffected by price fluctuations of the underlying securities.

Stock selection risk. Exposure to uncertainty about the future valuation of a particular stock.

Stock swap merger. A deal in which the holders of the target company's stock receive shares of the acquiring company's stock rather than cash.

Strategic acquisition. A generally noncompetitive situation in which the acquiring company has a good business reason for the merger, such as expanding product capability.

Structural anomalies. Greater-than-expected price discounts that can be attributed to nonmarket or nonrational technical factors.

Systematic or market risk. Exposure to uncertainty about systematic rises and falls in stock market prices that affect the prices of all stocks in a market or sector.

Systematic risk factors. Factors, such as interest rates or the price of oil, that have the ability to affect systematically the valuation of a whole range of stocks if they change.

Time horizon analysis. The examination of the time frame for completion of a corporate event (if the event is going to happen, then when will it occur?).

Trading positions. Opportunistic positions designed to take advantage of short-term market mispricings and inefficiencies rather than hedge against market decline.

Warrant. The stock conversion component of a convertible bond.

Within the hedge. A phrase used to describe that portion of an equity hedge portfolio in which long positions are matched by equal dollar amounts of short positions.

Yield. The single investment rate that sets the present value of all a bond's future cash payments equal to the price of the bond.

NOTES

INTRODUCTION

1 All analysis and performance statistics provided in this book are based on Hedge Fund Research, Inc. performance indices. Appendix A explains the calculation methodology and definitions of important variables; Appendix B lists further resources, and Appendix C is hedge fund research performance indices.

2 George Soros, *Soros on Soros: Staying Ahead of the Curve* (New York: John Wiley and Sons, 1995), 68.

CHAPTER 1

3 Carol J. Loomis, "The Jones Nobody Keeps Up With," *Fortune* (1962): 237–47

CHAPTER 3

4 Chapter based on paper presented at the Hedge Fund Research, Inc. conference on Alternative Investments, University of Chicago, 22 July, 1998. Stephanie Breslow of Schultz, Roth and Zabel, L.L.P., "Legal Issues in Connection with Investments by Tax-Exempt Entities in Hedge Funds, Other Investment Funds, and Managed Accounts."

CHAPTER 4

5 Paul Upcraft, personal correspondence to author, 20 July, 1998.

CHAPTER 5

6 John Brush, Ph.D., personal correspondence to author 20 July, 1998.

7 Edward L. Finn, personal correspondence to author, 22 July, 1998.

8 Christopher Luck, personal correspondence to author, 15 July, 1998.

CHAPTER 6

9 Thomas Noddings, personal correspondence to author, 17 July, 1998.

CHAPTER 7

10 George Kellner, personal correspondence to author, 17 July, 1998.

11 Based on an exchange ratio of 1.75 on 13 June, 1997.

CHAPTER 8

12 Brian Higgins, personal correspondence to author, 14 July, 1998.

CHAPTER 9

13 James Dinan, President of JGD Management Corporation, "Event-Driven Strategies" (paper presented at the Hedge Fund Research, Inc. conference on Alternative Investments, University of Chicago, 22 July, 1998).

CHAPTER 10

14 Soros, 71-77.

15 Dinan.

CHAPTER 11

16 Peter Kash, personal correspondence to author, 17 July, 1998.

17 Dale Jacobs, personal correspondence to author, 17 July, 1998.

CHAPTER 12

18 Cappy R. McGarr, personal correspondence to author, 14 July, 1998.

19 Ron Pollack, personal correspondence to author, 18 July, 1998.

INDEX

ABOUT BLOOMBERG

Bloomberg L.P., founded in 1981, is a global information services, news, and media company. Headquartered in New York, the company has nine sales offices, two data centers, and 87 news bureaus worldwide.

Bloomberg, serving customers in 126 countries around the world, holds a unique position within the financial services industry by providing an unparalleled range of features in a single package, the BLOOMBERG PROFESSIONAL® service. By addressing the demand for investment performance and efficiency through an exceptional combination of information, analytic, electronic trading, and Straight Through Processing tools, Bloomberg has built a worldwide customer base of corporations, issuers, financial intermediaries, and institutional investors.

BLOOMBERG NEWS®, founded in 1990, provides stories and columns on business, general news, politics, and sports to leading newspapers and magazines throughout the world. BLOOMBERG TELEVISION®, a 24-hour business and financial news network, is produced and distributed globally in seven different languages. BLOOMBERG RADIO℠ is an international radio network anchored by flagship station BLOOMBERG® WBBR 1130 in New York.

In addition to the BLOOMBERG PRESS® line of books, Bloomberg publishes *BLOOMBERG MARKETS™*, *BLOOMBERG PERSONAL FINANCE®*, and *BLOOMBERG WEALTH MANAGER®*. To learn more about Bloomberg, call a sales representative at:

Frankfurt:	49-69-92041-280	Singapore:	65-6212-1100
Hong Kong:	852-2977-6900	Sydney:	612-9777-8686
London:	44-20-7330-7500	Tokyo:	813-3201-8910
New York:	1-212-318-2200		
San Francisco:	1-415-912-2970		
São Paulo:	5511-3048-4506		

ABOUT THE AUTHOR

Joseph G. Nicholas is a leading authority on hedge funds and alternative investment strategies. Mr. Nicholas is Founder and Chairman of HFR Group, LLC, which includes HFR Asset Management, LLC, a fund-of-funds management company, HFR Europe, Ltd, an investment advisory firm, and Hedge Fund Research, Inc., a leading supplier of data on hedge funds, including the HFR Databases, the industry's largest and most comprehensive hedge fund databases. Mr. Nicholas is author of *Market-Neutral Investing: Long/Short Hedge Fund Strategies* (Bloomberg Press), is a frequent lecturer on topics relating to alternative investments, and has appeared on CNN and *Nightly Business Report*. Mr. Nicholas received a Bachelor of Science Degree in Commerce from DePaul University and the degree of Juris Doctor from Northwestern University School of Law.